Uncommon Questions from an Extraordinary Savior

Christopher Bozung

Energion Publications
P. O. Box 841
Gonzalez, FL 32560

energionpubs.com

Cover Design: Christopher Bozung
Author Photo: Christian Bozung

ISBN10: 1-938434-06-4
ISBN13: 978-1-938434-06-8
Library of Congress Control Number: 2012949736

To my children,
Christian, Arriana, Cashmira, and Chase
who taught me no question is beyond asking

TABLE OF CONTENTS

FOREWORD

Have you ever questioned what Jesus questioned? Have you ever thought about what Jesus was thinking? Have you ever wondered what Jesus wondered about? If only we could know his questions. But we can! Jesus was the master questioner of history.

Jesus asked questions on approximately 115 different occasions. And yet, as Chris Bozung asserts, the Savior's questions are truly unique. That's the premise of his book, *Uncommon Questions from an Extraordinary Savior*.

A decade ago while visiting Regent University in Virginia Beach, Chris asked me to sign a copy of my own book, *Soul Tsunami*. While I was autographing the inside cover, he said, "I'm working on a book that asserts that Jesus never asked a question because he needed to know the answer."

It was an intriguing thought, a thought that I couldn't shake off when a few months later I picked up for the first time *Letters to a Young Poet* (New York: W. W. Norton, 1934). These ten letters were written by the Bohemian-Austrian poet Rainer Maria Rilke (1875-1926) to a young man named Franz Xaver Kappus (age 19) about to enter the German military. Kappus sought advice from the senior Rilke (age 27) on what it means to be an artist and a human being. My favorite letter is this one dated 16 July 1903:

> You are so young, so before all beginning, and I want to beg you, as much as I can, dear sir, to be patient towards all that is unsolved in your heart and to try to love the questions themselves like locked rooms and like books that are written

in a very foreign tongue. Do not now seek the answers, that cannot be given you because you would not be able to live them. And the point is, to live everything. LIVE the questions now. Perhaps you will then gradually, without noticing it, live along some distant day into the answer (33-34).

Chris got me thinking about what it might mean to live the questions of Jesus. What can be learned from examining the questions of Jesus? What is true about any single question of Jesus, yet true about all the questions of Jesus at the same time? Stated simply, what do His questions have in common?

Chris' book overflows with astute perceptions on Jesus' mode of questioning. His starting point is bold yet simple: Jesus asked questions in a way no one before or since has ever done. He contends that with Jesus, we never have to wonder whether the correct question was being asked. Chris asserts Jesus did not ask questions simply to gather information or secure facts. He writes from the perspective that Jesus' use of questions emphasized inward change in those Jesus' was questioning.

I came away from this book realizing that Jesus didn't ask questions to get an answer so much as to provoke a re-start. Sometimes certain areas of our lives need restarts more than answers. I did not know how much I needed this book until after I read it.

Chris' concept is fresh, different, solid, and interesting. His book includes provocative interactions to get small groups to ask great questions. As you read *Uncommon Questions* I hope you'll agree that Jesus never asked a question because he needed to know the answer.

Leonard Sweet
Madison, New Jersey

"Oh my soul ... be prepared to meet him who knows how to ask questions."
T.S. Eliot, *The Rock*

INTRODUCTION

In Chicago, March 1992, an 8-year-old boy was questioned by police after he shot a girl classmate in the spine with a semiautomatic handgun. *"Is this going to take long?"* he asked the detectives, *"I've got someplace to go tonight."*[1]

Questions define our thoughts. They are used to attract the attention of the listener and prejudice responses. They help us to build our understanding of a subject or idea. Yet not all questions challenge us in the same way. Open-ended questions require much thought. Closed-ended questions require a simple "yes" or "no." Rhetorical questions have self-evident answers. Hypothetical questions ask us to begin the process of thinking and answering.

Have you ever noticed how many questions *you* ask in a day – or perhaps someone asks you?

In just one hour's time, my son Christian asked me, *"Why are your lips red? Where does your tongue go when you close your mouth? How do they make potato chips? Why do we only have ten fingers?"* My daughter Arriana – who tends to be more pragmatic – asked me, *"Do old people take a shower?"*

Since I first began studying the questions of Jesus, I have collected questions people ask. Here are some of my favorites:

Why do they lock gas station rest rooms? Are they afraid someone will clean them?

Do vegetarians eat animal crackers?

Why isn't there mouse-flavored cat food?

What was the best thing before sliced bread?

Two of the best questions, though, come from the presidential election of 1948 in which Governor Thomas Dewey lost to Harry S Truman. Paul Boller writes in *Presidential Anecdotes*, "Stunned by his defeat, Dewey later said he felt like the man who woke up to find himself inside a coffin with a lily in his hand and thought to himself: *'If I'm alive, what am I doing here? And if I'm dead, why do I have to go to the bathroom?'*"[2]

The pages of the New Testament contain some 340 individual questions Jesus asked. Such questions as:

"Why were you searching for me?" "Didn't you know that I had to be in my Father's house?" "Who are my mother and my brothers?"

"Now which of them will love him more?" "Simon son of John, do you truly love me?"

"Why are you so afraid?" "Do you still have no faith?"

"Which is easier: to say, 'Your sins are forgiven,' or to say, 'Get up and walk'?" "Do you want to get well?"

"Who do people say that I am?" "Why do you call me, 'Lord, Lord,' and do not do what I say?"

"What are you discussing together as you walk along?" "Did not the Christ have to suffer these things and then enter his glory?"

"What good will it be for a man if he gains the whole world, yet forfeits his soul?" "Or what can a man give in exchange for his soul?" "Friends, haven't you any fish?"

"My God, my God, why have you forsaken me?"

These are questions formed on the lips of the very Son of God. Was he merely gathering facts or simply introducing a story? Did Jesus ask questions for the same reasons we ask them? Or is there more behind the questions of Jesus than meets the eye?

Jesus knew the hearts of man as only a Divine One can. His omniscience, his knowledge of the thoughts of those to whom he directed his questions – are characteristics that can never be duplicated by any mortal man.

The questions Jesus asked capture his thoughts about his own ministry, teachings, and dealings with both man and God. His ability to ask the *right question* at the *right moment* for the *right need* will be unmatched by anyone. His questions can only be mimicked in a crude fashion. His skill in crafting a question to pierce the heart, to quicken the thoughts, to convict the conscience, to elicit faith – those are abilities that are only occasionally, if ever, stumbled upon in the discourse between men. His questions were truly unique because Jesus was unique. *They are uncommon questions from an extraordinary Savior.*

The Premise:
(upon which this book is written)

Jesus never asked a question because
he needed to know the answer

"The one who asks questions
doesn't lose his way."
African Proverb

Part I:
The Journey Begins

I

WHERE CAN I FIND JESUS?
The Question of Discovery

Every year his parents went to Jerusalem for the Feast of the Passover. When he was twelve years old, they went up to the Feast, according to the custom. After the Feast was over, while his parents were returning home, the boy Jesus stayed behind in Jerusalem, but they were unaware of it. Thinking he was in their company, they traveled on for a day. Then they began looking for him among their relatives and friends. When they did not find him, they went back to Jerusalem to look for him. After three days they found him in the temple courts, sitting among the teachers, listening to them and asking them questions. Everyone who heard him was amazed at his understanding and his answers. When his parents saw him, they were astonished. His mother said to him, "Son, why have you treated us like this? Your father and I have been anxiously searching for you."

"Why were you searching for me?" *he asked.* **"Didn't you know I had to be in my Father's house?"** *But they did not understand what he was saying to them.*

Then he went down to Nazareth with them and was obedient to them. But his mother treasured all these things in her heart.
~Luke 2:41-51

Taylor Touchstone, an autistic twelve year old, was missing. His parents were wild with worry. Neighbors, friends and officials searched for four days until they found him naked and hungry in a swamp fourteen miles from where he disappeared. He was hospitalized in good condition: a story with a happy ending.

You read about it all the time. A child lost; a parent concerned. The community rallies together. The child is found; the parent is relieved.

It's never that simple, though. All the words in the world can't capture what a parent feels during those moments when his or her own child is lost. Mary, who alone does the talking, asks her son – *the Son* – the question only a concerned parent can ask. *"Son, why have you treated us like this? Your father and I have been anxiously searching for you."*

"Why were you searching for me ... Didn't you know that I had to be in my Father's house?" Scripture records these as the first questions Jesus asked. The story is fairly straightforward. Mary and Joseph can't find Jesus. They look high and low throughout Jerusalem, only to discover that the whole time Jesus was at the temple sitting, listening, asking, and answering.

JEN IS IN *BIG TROUBLE!*

When I was eleven years old, my family moved from New Jersey to Pennsylvania. On moving day, the moving people came to pack and load all our belongings.

When you were growing up, do you remember *being around your parents* when a sibling disappeared into thin air? You know – *suddenly was nowhere to be found?* I grew up with five brothers and sisters, so more times than I can remember we all ran around the neighborhood looking for one of my siblings who seemed to vanish. At some point, one of my parents – *usually my mom* – always said something to the effect that when we found whoever it was that had magically disappeared, they were in *Big Trouble*. Of course, that always made me wonder if there was an advantage in *staying* lost. Being in *Big Trouble* meant they would be glad to find us, but not so overjoyed that they wouldn't spank us for getting lost in the first place!

Which brings me back to our move to Pennsylvania. When the moving truck was nearly loaded, my parents discovered that my youngest sister, Jen, was missing. My mom announced – to no surprise of those drafted to the newly formed Search Party – that when we found my sister, she would be in *Big Trouble*.

We eventually found Jen in her bedroom, asleep in her closet, *on a shelf.* By then my parents didn't have the heart to wake her and spank her.

Now, I'm making light of a serious situation, *but at the time, no one laughed.* Everyone was running around and everyone was serious.

"Why have you treated us like this?" Jesus' mother asks. Was she anxious? Of course. Was she upset? Better believe it. Was she laughing? No way!

Note the enormous contrast between his parents' great concern for him, and Jesus' lack of concern for them. Jesus – in a *reversal* he will use many times again in the Gospels – answers Mary's question with a question. Not just one, but two. **"Why were you searching for me? Didn't you know that I had to be in my Father's house?"**

One truth I discovered as I studied the questions of Jesus is this: *Jesus never asked a question because <u>he needed to know the answer.</u>* In other words, not once did Jesus ask a question because he needed to know the answer. This principle is at the heart of understanding Jesus' questions.

Jesus' use of questions emphasized inward change. What do I mean? Jesus' questions were designed to *effect change in the hearer.* In other words, *Jesus was asking the question entirely for the benefit of the listener.*

ᏬᏋᏋᏬ

Jesus never asked a question because he needed to know the answer.

ᏬᏋᏋᏬ

HAND-HELD GAMES & BULLDOZERS

If I suddenly discovered while driving back home from Wal-Mart that I left my son Christian behind, I would turn the car around and go back to look for him.

Where would I look for him first? *The electronics section.* If I lost Chase, the first place I'd look for him would be *the truck aisle.*

Why?

Because I know my children.

☙❧

A proper understanding of where to find Jesus begins with understanding who he is.

☙❧

A proper understanding of where to find Jesus begins with understanding who he is.

If anyone should have understood, Mary and Joseph should have. Couldn't they recall the visits by angelic hosts just twelve years before?[3] Didn't they remember the Magi bearing gifts for the Christ-Child?[4] Was the divine protection from Herod's sword so soon forgotten?[5]

But Luke tells us they didn't understand. Why didn't they understand? *Why didn't they know where to find Jesus?* Because they didn't understand who he was!

The temple was the last place they looked. Why? Because they did not yet completely understand who he was. His questioning of them – **"Why ... Didn't you know?"** – implies they should have understood who he was. *"But they did not understand what he was saying to them,"* Luke tells his readers.

That may sound a little harsh. Perhaps we're more comfortable with saying they lost sight of who he was. But the truth is – just as with you and me – Mary and Joseph needed a personal encounter with the promised Messiah, *Truth Personified.* They were not exempt from needing salvation and the understanding that *their son* was the Savior.

This is a difficult passage for some to understand. Difficult in the sense that it is hard for us to understand the actions and words of Jesus. Was Jesus proper in what he did?

Explain his words and actions any way you like, *but don't explain them as sin.* We must not think of what Jesus did as disobedient or mischievous. For we know Jesus was without sin. So explain them anyway you want, but however you choose to describe Jesus' dealings, you cannot see them as sin.

And that's why the passage is difficult for some to understand. It is a hard thing to swallow – not that Jesus didn't sin (we accept that) – but we somehow would like to think Jesus did *something* wrong by staying behind in Jerusalem.

But he didn't.

SURPRISE!!!

Before I married my wife, I naively thought I knew almost everything about her. After we were married three years, I was *convinced* I knew everything about her. One day we were sitting at the table enjoying lunch together. *And then it happened.* She said to me, "I'll bet you didn't know I could juggle."

"No way," I said. "That can't be!" So she went to the refrigerator, took out three oranges, and proceeded to show me something I never knew about the woman I'd been married to for three whole years! I discovered I didn't know my wife as well as I thought I did.

How well do you know Jesus? Do you know him as well as you think you do?

Mary and Joseph knew Jesus better than anyone else. They lived in the same house as Jesus, the Son of God. Yet, they didn't know him fully. They knew him as their son, but not as *the* Son. They knew what they'd been told by angels, but they didn't know *that which angels never experience* – knowing Jesus as Savior.

Where can you find Jesus? You can find him in the pages of Scripture. Colossians tells us he was the one who created the world![6]

That's an awesome thought: the one who created the world also came to live among us.

Where can you find Jesus? You won't find him at the Temple. But if you believe he is the Son of God – that he died for you – he'll come and live in the temple of your heart.

If you don't know Jesus as Savior, tell him you want to know him. Ask him to forgive you of your sins. Tell him you believe he died for you.

MY STORY

Thirty-five years ago, as a young teenager, I asked Jesus into my heart. I can't tell you the date; I only know it was the summer of my fifteenth year. Up to that point, I spent my entire life going to a church, which taught *about* Jesus. But never once during all those years had someone taught me *where* to find Jesus. What I had was *head-knowledge* about the person of Jesus. But what I needed was *heart-knowledge* about the work of Jesus on the Cross as it related to my life.

Do you know where to find Jesus? How well do you *really* know him?

Luke concludes: *"Then he went down to Nazareth with them and was obedient to them."* A story with a happy ending.

And so the journey begins. Do you know where to find Jesus? It's a question of discovery.

Prayer

Lord God, I think I know you. I want to believe I know you as well as I can. Is it possible that I – like Jesus' own mother and father – don't know you as well as I should? Help me to know you, God. Open my eyes to you. Help me to see you for who you are and not for whom I have made you out to be. I want Jesus to come into my heart right now. I want to know him as more than just a good teacher or a prophet. I want to see what Mary and Joseph could not see. I want to see Jesus as the Savior – as my Savior. Amen.

Talking Points

1. Did it ever occur to you that Mary and Joseph lost Jesus? The very ones entrusted with his safety, lost him. But this question is not about losing him. It's about finding him. It's about discovering who Jesus is. What does it mean to discover who Jesus is?

2. Even if you think you know someone, it's easy to be surprised by something you never knew about that person. The longer you know the person, the more surprising a revelation can be. Has God taught you anything about himself recently that has surprised you?

2

WHAT IF MY FAMILY THINKS I'M CRAZY?
The Question of Opposition

Jesus entered a house, and again a crowd gathered, so that he and his disciples were not even able to eat. When his family heard about this, they went to take charge of him, for they said, "He is out of his mind."

Then Jesus' mother and brothers arrived. Standing outside, they sent someone in to call him. A crowd was sitting around him, and they told him, "Your mother and brothers are outside looking for you."

***"Who are my mother and my brothers?"** he asked.*

Then he looked at those seated in a circle around him and said, "Here are my mother and my brothers! Whoever does God's will is my brother and sister and mother."

~Mark 3:20-21, 31-35

While Jesus immersed himself in ministry, pouring his time into others and teaching his disciples, his family heard a report that he was neglecting himself and not eating properly. So they decided to go get him and take him home.

Mark shows us a glimpse into the opposition Jesus faced even from his own family. You may be familiar with it.

It's a question many Christians struggle with. *My family thinks I'm a religious fanatic! What can I say to them? How can I make them see what I see? If only they would believe!*

Facing opposition for believing in Jesus is not easy – especially if the opposition is your family.

All too often a person accepts Christ only to see his family make fun of him – or worse, have nothing to do with him.

What an embarrassment! What a nut! Look what he's doing to the family name!

One of the verses in this passage has quite an interesting history. Verse 21 states, *'When his family heard about this, they went to take charge of him, for they said, "He is out of his mind."'* The centuries have seen many changes, additions, and subtractions to the original version, mostly related to interpretation of the original Greek. Depending on which translation you read, the text differs when it comes to *who it was who actually heard the report about Jesus.*

For example, the New International Version (the version we're now reading) states, "When his *family* heard about this…" The King James Version says, "And when *his friends* heard of it…" The Modern Language translation reads, "When *His relatives* learned of it…" And The New King James Version states, "But when *His own people* heard…"

These various translations show the tension between seeing Jesus as the *Son of God*, and hearing his family call him *crazy*. It's somehow easier to think that Jesus' *friends or relatives* might have seen him as off his rocker, than to think *his own family* did.

But ten verses later Mark informs us that those who came to take charge of him were his mother and brothers. John tells us in his Gospel, "even his own brothers did not believe in him."[8]

Since Joseph is *not* mentioned here – and hasn't been heard from since Jesus was twelve years old – most scholars assume he was no longer alive at that time. The pressure from Jesus' family was nonetheless real.

So I have no doubt that it was Jesus' family – his mother and brothers – who came to get him.

It reminds me of the proverbial 'straw that broke the camel's back.' Imagine it:

ᎶᏋᎧᎧ

What do you do when your family stands opposed to your devotion to the Lord? How do you answer their concerns?

ᎶᏋᎧᎧ

first, a good, respectable carpenter who doesn't carry on the family business. Then he runs around with a group of guys who are all religious freaks. Worse than that, some of them are fishermen and tax collectors. To top it all off, he thinks he's God!

What do you do when your family stands opposed to your devotion to the Lord? How do you answer their concerns? Their hostility?

DOUG GOES OFF TO COLLEGE

I remember when my older brother Doug came to a saving knowledge of Jesus Christ – the first in our family to do so. He was in college at the time. And when he came home and explained the change in his life because of Jesus, my Dad reacted violently. He pounded his fist on the dinner table and told my brother in so many words he would stand for none of this "Jesus" stuff. (And that from a man who religiously brought his family to church every Sunday.)

Jesus wasn't sitting down at the dining room table with his dad when he began his ministry. But at some point in his ministry, his family decided they weren't going to stand for all this "religious" stuff. Mark tells us, *'When his family heard about this, they went to take charge of him, for they said, "He is out of his mind."'*

The phrase *"they went to take charge of him"* is seven words long in our English Bible – but just three words in the original Greek. The verb translated *take charge* is used several others times in the Mark's Gospel: *"For Herod himself had given orders to have John **arrested**... Then they looked for a way to **arrest** him[10]...the chief priests and the teachers of the law were looking for some sly way to **arrest** Jesus and kill him[11]... The men seized Jesus and **arrested** him..."[12]*

Jesus' family did not intend to arrest him in the same way Herod would later arrest him, but the idea carried by the Greek verb is that they were determined to take him against his will.

Why do they want to take charge of him? Mark says, "He is out of his mind." Literally, he is crazy! That's pretty severe. Imagine your own family ready to commit you! (It's the same thing said of the Apostle Paul in the Book of Acts when King Agrippa accused Paul of being out of his mind.)[13]

Then Jesus' mother and brothers arrived. Standing outside, they sent someone in to call him.

Jesus' family arrives. It is so crowded, they can't get in the house where Jesus is teaching. But word gets in that they are outside. *They're here and they're determined to take Jesus home.*

So what *do you do* when your family stands opposed to you and "religion"? *What if* your family thinks you're crazy? And it's not just confined to family. Sometimes it is our coworkers, or our neighbors. Sometimes it's old friends, those we previously ran around with, but now they think we're nuts.

"Who are my mother and my brothers?" *Jesus asked. This straightforward question is quite profound considering it is Jesus who is asking.* How did he answer the question? He knew *why* his family stood outside. He knew they hadn't brought him a warm meal and an extra change of clothes. They opposed Jesus' choices because they didn't believe in him. How did he deal with their unbelief?

The answer is simple. *'***"Who are my mother and my brothers?"** *he asked. Then he looked at those seated in a circle around him ...'* Matthew's Gospel says Jesus pointed to his disciples and said, "Here are my mother and my brothers."[14]

The disciples were certainly doing God's will (Judas too) by sitting there with Jesus, asking questions and learning from a teacher thought to be crazy by his own family. These disciples entered into a relationship with Jesus that went beyond family ties.

ଚ୧୨ଚ

Being a disciple of Jesus means doing the will of God – whatever the cost.

ଚ୧୨ଚ

To Jesus, those who saw things through his Father's eyes were his true family. It doesn't mean he loved his earthly family any less. But it also doesn't mean he wavered from his commitment to the will of his heavenly Father.

Being a disciple of Jesus means doing the will of God – whatever the cost. Sometimes following Jesus means forsaking family. Is your family's view of your love for God less than ideal? Do you find yourself defending your words and actions to your brother, or sister, or mother, or father?

Take comfort in the fact that Jesus has been where you are. Just as with Jesus, it may be that your family doesn't know how to express their concern for you. C.L. Mitton said this about the words used by Jesus' family:

"If they reveal his family's failure to understand him, they are also a measure of their concern for him."

Being a disciple of Jesus means being willing to have your family misjudge your motives and oppose your actions. They may question *why* you go to church. They may question *where* you go to church. They may call you names and joke behind your back.

While some of it is intentional, some of it comes from their inability to express to us their concern for us. There is no doubt they love us! But they just don't know how to tell us that they are worried about what we've gotten into.

*"**Who are my mother and my brothers?"** Then he looked at those seated in a circle around him ...'* You are. You are when you do his will. Jesus is right there with you.

And no one on earth can take that from you.

> Being a disciple of Jesus means being willing to have your family misjudge your motives and oppose your actions.

Prayer

God, you know my heart. You know that I want to follow you more than anything. But at times my family and friends make it very difficult to love them when they oppose my faith. Give me the strength I need to follow you and put up with the opposition while keeping my witness (all at the same time!). Amen.

Talking Points

1. Being a disciple of Jesus might mean your family or friends will misjudge your motives and oppose your actions. Does it bring you comfort to know Jesus was opposed by his family?

2. Is there truth in the statement, 'your family may oppose you simply because they don't know how to express their concern for you?' Why or why not?

3

How Much Does He Ask of Me?
The Question of Commitment

From that time on Jesus began to explain to his disciples that he must go to Jerusalem and suffer many things at the hands of the elders, chief priests and teachers of the law, and that he must be killed and on the third day be raised to life.

Peter took him aside and began to rebuke him. "Never, Lord!" he said. "This shall never happen to you!"

Jesus turned and said to Peter, "Get behind me, Satan! You are a stumbling block to me; you do not have in mind the things of God, but the things of men."

Then Jesus said to his disciples, "If anyone would come after me, he must deny himself and take up his cross and follow me. For whoever wants to save his life will lose it, but whoever loses his life for me will find it. **What good will it be for a man if he gains the whole world, yet forfeits his soul? Or what can a man give in exchange for his soul?"**

~Matthew 16:21-26

Perhaps the hardest thing for the disciples to accept was the idea that Jesus was going to die. When Jesus first began to explain this to them, Peter took him aside in order to set him straight. For Peter and the others, Jesus was the one who was going to set up the Kingdom! Peter wouldn't hear of Jesus suffering, let alone being killed! It wasn't part of Peter's plan – for himself, or Jesus.

But Jesus knew that part of the Father's plan involved his own death. Peter, Jesus explained, had the things of man in mind, not the things of God.

If one is to be totally committed to God – totally sold out – he needs to have in mind the things of God.

'PROTEIN DRINK, ANYONE?'

One of the things we like to do a lot at our house is make protein drinks. But with six in our family, it's quite the process. To begin, we have to get out the orange juice; if there is not enough, we have to mix up some more. We then need to mix the protein powder in the blender with the orange juice, some ice, and half a banana. We then get out six glasses, and six straws. The blender never holds enough, so we have to repeat the entire process twice. When we are done, the blender needs to be cleaned out, the spilled powder wiped off the counter, and the juice put back into the fridge.

The other day Arriana asked her mother if she could make protein drinks. My wife replied, *"If you want them, you make them!"* In order for Arriana to *really* want a protein drink, *she has to be totally committed.*

Being totally committed means denying oneself. Being totally committed means taking up one's cross – making *his* will *your* will. The world calls us to live our own dreams, to do what *we* want. The world tells us, "Look out for number one!" and "You're worth it!"

But Jesus says, "If you want to keep your life, lose it." That's radical. That goes against everything society tells me. It goes against everything common sense tells me.

And then Jesus asks two questions. **"What good will it be for a man if he gains the whole world, yet forfeits his soul? Or what can a man give in exchange for his soul?"**

They're rhetorical questions. Questions not meant to be an-swered out loud. They're questions to be answered within one's heart. Questions to be personalized. "What *will* it profit me if I gain the whole world, yet lose my soul?"

"Nothing!" my inner voice replies, "If I forfeit my soul, I've lost. Even gaining the whole world means nothing if I lose my soul."

Jesus says, "Give it to me! Give me your life. You want to be committed to me? Give me everything. Don't hold back!" You see, as far as the Savior is concerned, you've lost the game of life if you forfeit your soul.

They're rhetorical questions. Questions not meant to be answered out loud. They're questions to be answered within one's heart.

It's not always easy to die to a dream. Giving up something, conforming to someone else's idea or expectation, or putting others before self can all be things we find difficult to do.

And when God is the one who is asking for the change in our life, obeying his will can be a struggle. Has God ever asked you to lose your life for him? Has he ever asked you to make his will your will?

How much does he ask of you? Are you willing to give up your soul in exchange for the whole world?

To Jesus, his cross was the Cross. What is your cross? How much does he ask

The question is really a question of commitment. How committed are you?

of you? The question is really a question of commitment. How committed are you? Are you standing in the way of his plan – a stumbling block like Peter on this occasion? Or are you sold out to Jesus?

It's easy to settle back into our relationship with the Lord and get comfortable. Too comfortable. And the things of the world become our focus. *"You do not have in mind the things of God, but the things of men."*

MY CELL PHONE

I lost my cell phone yesterday. I found it today, so the story ends well. But for the time it was lost, I was upset. I re-traced every step I took; I even looked in some places *twice.* You've done that, I'm sure. I looked twice in my office, twice in my van, twice in the garage. I searched the entire house three times. And then I got a novel idea: *why don't I call the phone and listen for it to ring?* You should have seen me calling the number and trying to listen for it *before* the voice mail kicked in after the fifth ring! After the third attempt at calling the phone, it occurred to me that I had turned the phone off!

I wonder if God ever tries to locate us *and we're "powered off" spiritually speaking.* When we get too comfortable with the world, our relationship with the Lord suffers. We turn off our communication with God and wonder why it seems like God never speaks to us.

Peter was out of touch with the plan that Jesus had for his own life. *There was a communication breakdown.*

Peter's understanding of what was expected of him and what he could expect of Jesus needed updating. When Peter was content to keep things going along as they always had, Jesus upped the requirements.

Jesus' announcement to the disciples that he was going to die on the Cross required, *demanded,* more of the disciples – as voiced by Peter – than they wanted to give. *It meant giving up Jesus.*

Our relationship with God – like Peter's – begins when we allow Jesus to go to the Cross for us. Sometimes things – whether they are tangible like a new car, or intangible, like the dream of owning our own business, stand in the way of us giving Jesus first priority in our life.

How much does he ask of you? Would you believe, *your very life?* Nothing less. He's not asking you to risk your investments, or your savings, or any worldly possession. (Besides, what good are they if you lose your very soul in the end?) He's asking you to risk your life. That doesn't mean you will suffer physically for him. But you may.[15] That doesn't mean you will die in service for him. But you may. It doesn't mean you'll have to go to the jungles of South America as a missionary. But you may.

The question is a question of commitment. ***"What good will it be for a man if he gains the whole world, yet forfeits his soul? Or what can a man give in exchange for his soul?"*** What good will it be for you to have anything other than what God wants for you? If we want to grow stronger in our relationship with Jesus, we need to stand ready to give God whatever he requires of us.

How much does he ask of you? The question is really a question of commitment. *How much will you give?*

Prayer

Father, forgive me for the times when I, like Peter, have tried to stand in the way of your plans – for me! I want my commitment to you to be strong. Help me to put my own selfish designs at your feet. Keep me from becoming a stumbling block to your plans for your Church or me. May you never allow my foolish thinking to deceive me into believing I can gain anything without being totally sold out to you. Amen.

Talking Points

1. With these questions Jesus asks, he is saying, 'if you are going to be my disciple, I want something.' What is it he's asking of you?

2. Jesus' sharp words to Peter in verse 23 – "Get behind me, Satan!" – are recorded by Matthew twelve chapters earlier. When Satan tried to tempt Jesus during the 40 days of temptation, Jesus rebuked Satan with, "Get behind me, Satan!" How easy is it to stand in the way of God's will for us, or his Church? Is there something you are doing which is making you an obstacle to God's perfect will?

"When we have arrived at the question,
the answer is already near."
Ralph Waldo Emerson

Part II:
Deepening Our Faith

4

Is It Okay To Ask God For A Miracle?
The Question of Inquiry

The next day Jesus decided to go to Galilee. He found Philip and said to him, "Follow me."

Now Philip was from Bethsaida, the city of Andrew and Peter. Philip found Nathanael and said to him, "We have found him about whom Moses in the law and also the prophets wrote, Jesus son of Joseph from Nazareth."

Nathanael said to him, "Can anything good come out of Nazareth?" Philip said to him, "Come and see."

When Jesus saw Nathanael coming toward him, he said of him, "Here is truly an Israelite in whom there is no deceit!"

Nathanael asked him, "Where did you get to know me?" Jesus answered, "I saw you under the fig tree before Philip called you."

Nathanael replied, "Rabbi, you are the Son of God! You are the King of Israel!"

Jesus answered, **"Do you believe because I told you that I saw you under the fig tree?**[16] *You will see greater things than these."*
~John 1:43-50 [NRSV]

John doesn't tell us the turn of events that led Nathanael to the shade of a fig tree. We don't know how long he was there or where the fig tree was. We don't even know how much distance was between him and the fig tree before Philip found him. But I'd like to believe Nathanael's *time-out* under the tree was known to no one but himself. *No one, that is, but the one who knows everything.*

Although Nathanael doesn't believe a word Philip says to him, he follows along grumbling that nothing good can come out of Nazareth.

HIGH SCHOOL FOOTBALL

I'm reminded of my youth in Pennsylvania, and the tremendous rivalry between my hometown high school football team and the neighboring town's football team. A person from my town did not dare wear a lettered jacket in the neighboring town. And the same was true of a varsity player from the neighboring town on our home turf!

So what Nathanael states here may represent a long-standing hostility between these two neighboring towns. He is right in one sense; the prophets never uttered a word about Nazareth. It's not even mentioned in the Torah or the Jewish writings. The Messiah was to be born in *Bethlehem*; almost everyone knew that. But *Nazareth? "Can anything good come out of Nazareth?"*

As Nathanael approached Jesus, Jesus remarked, *"Here is a true Israelite, in whom there is nothing false."* The word *false* is translated *guile* in some Bibles. The word itself means deceit and earlier Greek writers had it describe anything deceiving or deceptive. (For example, in Greek literature it is used to describe the Trojan horse.)

David describes the *guileless* man in Psalm 15: *'LORD, who may dwell in your sanctuary? Who may live on your holy hill? He whose walk is blameless and who does what is righteous, who speaks the truth from his heart and has no slander on his tongue, who does his neighbor no wrong and casts no slur on his fellow man, who despises a vile man but honors those who fear the LORD, who keeps his oath even when it hurts, who lends his money without usury and does not accept a bribe against the innocent. He who does these things will never be shaken.* [17]

Jesus, of course, is not using *guile* in the negative sense of Nathanael.

So why mention it at all?

The answer may lie in what Nathanael was *doing* under the fig tree? What *was* Nathanael doing under the tree?

Some people picture Nathanael studying or reading or perhaps mediating on the promised Messiah. When Philip says to him, *"We have found the one Moses wrote about in the Law, and about whom the prophets also wrote – Jesus of Nazareth, the son of Joseph..."* Nathanael would have already had the promised Redeemer on the forefront of his thoughts.

I'd like to think Nathanael was reading from the first book of the Torah: Genesis. Genesis 25-32 to be exact. Those chapters describe *Jacob.* Let me summarize what they say about him: Jacob tricked his father Isaac and older brother Esau, connived Esau of his birthright, and then stole Isaac's blessing meant for Esau by dressing up like the older son![18]

In the same section of Genesis, God changes Jacob's name to *Israel.* So when Jesus says, "Here is a true Israelite, in whom there is nothing false" he's comparing Nathanael to Jacob.

But Nathanael differs from Jacob in one important sense: although Nathanael scoffs at the idea that something good can come from Nazareth, he did not refuse Philip's invitation to "come and see" like the bulk of Jacob's descendents (the nation of Israel) who hardened their hearts. Although Nathanael doubts Philip, he does follow him. And that differs radically from the way many in Israel reacted toward Jesus.

Nathanael, quite surprised to learn that Jesus knows him asks, *"Where did you get to know me?"* Jesus answers with a totally unexpected answer. *"I saw you under the fig tree before Philip called you."*

Then Nathanael believes. But not until Jesus told him he'd seen him sitting under the tree.

Jesus answered, **"Do you believe because I told you that I saw you under the fig tree?** *You will see greater things than these."* In other words, *'You think that's a big deal? You ain't seen nothing yet!'*

Nathanael believed because Jesus told him something Jesus could not possibly have known unless he was everything Philip claimed. Nathanael believed because Jesus told him he saw him under the tree.

It took a miracle before Nathanael would believe! In other words, *Nathanael didn't believe until he saw.*

Perhaps we can identify with Nathanael more than we'd like to admit. Are you sitting under a fig tree, waiting for God to see you? Do you refuse to believe unless God notices you on your terms?

How much does God have to do before we believe? How much does God have to say to us before we take him at his word?

ᏩᏋᎨᎣ

How much does God have to say to us before we take him at his word?

ᏩᏋᎨᎣ

When cancer strikes, when someone's marriage teeters on the brink of divorce, when someone faces insurmountable pain, they look for a miracle. We all hope for miracles under these circumstances.

Is there anything wrong with looking for a miracle? Even King Herod wanted to see Jesus perform a miracle.[19] (Jesus refused to do it!)[20]

RAIN, RAIN, GO AWAY!

In the Old Testament there was a man named Gideon who heard from God. God told him something and it should have ended there. But it wasn't enough for Gideon and it didn't end there. Gideon could not trust God at his word.

So what did Gideon do? He devised a plan to test whether he could trust God.[21] Before he went to sleep, he put some wool on the ground and asked God to make the wool wet and the ground under it dry. God did it. But again, it was not good enough for Gideon. So the next night Gideon asked God to make the ground wet and the wool dry. And God did that too.

What was Gideon looking for? He was looking for a miracle. Now catch this: he was looking for a miracle after God clearly spoke and revealed to Gideon what he was supposed to do.[22] Even though

God *did* answer through a miracle (the fleece being wet first while the ground was dry, and then the ground being wet while the fleece was dry), it showed a tremendous *lack of faith* on Gideon's part to ask for a sign to back up what God said to him.

Sometimes Gideon is held up as an example of what we should do when we want to find out what God wants us to do: *Should I go to this college? Should I marry this person? Should I take the job transfer across the country?*

Is it okay to ask God for a miracle? If you need a miracle to believe, no! Jesus desires for our faith in him be built upon his Word. Faith in Jesus should not need a sign or miracle to validate it. If we believe only if we see a miracle, it's really no faith at all!

Jesus said, *"Blessed are those who have not seen and yet have believed."*[23]

Is it okay to ask God for a miracle? If you believe God is still the God of miracles, yes! Nothing pleases the Father more than for his children to ask believing.

If we believe only if we see a miracle, it's really no faith at all!

Jesus also said, *"Therefore I tell you, whatever you ask for in prayer, believe that you have received it, and it will be yours."*[24]

Prayer

God in heaven, help me to take you at your word without testing you as Gideon did. Help me to trust you without seeking a sign or miracle as Nathanael did. Help my faith to grow as I build my relationship with you. Thank you for the Bible that helps me know what direction I should take when I'm trying to figure out which way to turn. Give me the boldness to seek out another godly man or woman whom I can talk to when I need counsel and wisdom. Amen.

Talking Points

1. *The desire to learn God's will for our life, the desire to have God validate our decisions is something all of us have from time to time. How can we be sure God wants us to do something without actually seeing him validate it?*

2. *The number of times Scripture records the sea parting or someone being raised from the dead can be counted on just a few fingers. Yet, we somehow have the idea God will use those extraordinary means to make his will known to us. What's wrong with requiring God to show us a miracle before we move forward?*

5

CAN WE HURRY GOD ALONG?
The Question of Involvement

On the third day a wedding took place at Cana in Galilee. Jesus'
mother was there, and Jesus and his disciples had also been invited to
the wedding. When the wine was gone, Jesus' mother said to him, "They
have no more wine."
"Dear woman, why do you involve me?" *Jesus replied, "My*
time has not yet come."
~John 2:1-4

When we open the pages of Scripture to *John 2*, we find ourselves at the beginning of Jesus' ministry. Jesus is at a wedding about
nine miles from his home town of Nazareth. He's with his family,
his brothers, and his mother.[25]

He'd called only five or six of his disciples, and they are with
him at the wedding. His ministry is still in the early stages of de-
veloping and the job of calling the rest of the disciples would come
later.

As of yet Jesus hadn't performed one public miracle or sign. If
we didn't know the rest of the story or the rest of John's Gospel, we
would have no reason to think he *could* or even *would* do a miracle.
Imagine that! What if Jesus *never did a miracle?*

And yet Mary turns to Jesus. *"They have no more wine."* So what
would make Mary think Jesus could or would do something about
the lack of wine? Did she know something others did not know?

Jesus' question implies she was expecting him to do something. What did she expect him to do? We cannot say with certainty, but *we* do know *she* knew miracles surrounded his conception and birth. When the angel Gabriel appeared to Mary to announce she was pregnant by the Holy Spirit[26] – that was nothing less than a miracle. When the angel appeared to Joseph and directed him not to divorce Mary even though the child was not his[27] – that was nothing less than a miracle. When angels announced Jesus' birth[28] and shepherds came[29] and then Magi[30] – those were nothing less than miracles.

But Jesus hadn't done these miracles himself directly, however. On one hand she *knew* all that. On the other hand, she displayed an incredible lack of understanding of who Jesus was when he disappeared during the trip to Jerusalem when he was a boy of twelve.[31]

And yet she looks to Jesus. *"They have no more wine."* If Jesus wanted to, this could be a great opportunity to make himself known! Surely a miracle would capture the people's attention. "They're out of wine! Call Jesus!" *Zap!* More wine! Think of the possibilities! Think of the headlines! *"Carpenter From Nazareth Produces Wine From Water. Some Call It A Miracle!"* Or *"Miracle Proves Messiah Has Come!"* But whose agenda would that be? Whose timetable?

ARE WE THERE YET?

"Are we there yet?" Any parent who's ever taken a trip longer than it takes to get to Wal-Mart has heard those words from the back seat of the car. Every year we take a trip to Florida to visit my parents who live there half the year. The trip is *long*. I know it's long and my wife knows it's long. The kids know it's long. *We take it every year.* Yet, without fail, every year someone from the back seat asks – within the first hour, mind you – "Are we there yet?"

I'm glad God doesn't mind us asking *him* the same question. From time to time when life seems to cave in around me, I ask him, "Are we there yet?" I know what he's going to say: the same thing I tell my children. "No! Enjoy the ride!" Enjoy the ride ... good advice for someone who's focused on the destination instead of the view.

John doesn't tell us *who* it is that's getting married, only that Jesus' mother is involving Jesus in something before he is ready to be involved.

For a number of years while working on my doctorate I worked in the student housing department of the school I attended. More times than I care to remember, a student's rent would come due. And there was no money to be had. The student would plead with the manager for more *time* and God for more *money*.

While the manager was usually quick to extend more time, God was not so quick to provide the much-needed revenue. But more times than not, I was amazed to learn that the rent money miraculously came in.

What is urgent to us may not be an emergency to God. Just because Mary is concerned they have run out of wine does not mean Jesus is concerned they have run out of wine. Jesus is not indifferent to the fact they've run out of wine. He's concerned that his mother is volunteering him for a job that would make his public identity as the Son of God known before he is ready to be known. *"Dear woman, why do you involve me? My time has not yet come."* She's hurrying him along!

⊙☯☯⊙

What is urgent to us may not be an emergency to God.

⊙☯☯⊙

Can we hurry God along? We'd like to think we can. After all, Jesus did what his mother asked by changing the water into wine. She turned to him, and he listened. She looked to him, and he answered. Jesus used the occasion to mark the beginning of his public miracles. Mary's request was honored, and the disciples put their faith in him.

God asks us to bring our concerns to him. *Cast your cares upon him, for he cares for you.*[32] It's not an easy thing to do. We'd rather take the short cut – the quick way out. That which we think is great material for a miracle, God does not choose to do anything with.

Can we hurry God along? *Mary did.* But it's not always that way. Sometimes it seems as if God doesn't want to be involved; that the *care* is ours alone. *We stand there shouting as loud as we can that there is no more wine!* But we're met with silence.

I'm convinced, however, it's in the *silence that we hear things we would never otherwise hear.* Things like patience. Things like long suffering. Things like "be still and know that I am God"[33] and "trust in me."[34]

Can we hurry God along? Jesus was not *forced* to change the water into wine. He did perform a miracle, but Mary did not compel Jesus to do anything *against his will.* And neither will we. *His ways are not our ways.* Sometimes our perspective is not his perspective. He is supreme. He is sovereign. It's his timetable, his agenda.

GᏋᎧᎧ

We stand there shouting as loud as we can that there is no more wine! But we're met with silence.

GᏋᎧᎧ

Wait patiently on the Lord.[35] Wait patiently on the Lord. Wait patiently on the Lord! That's what we hear more often than we'd like to admit.

That's our responsibility. *That's our concern.*

Are you facing a situation where God seems to be taking his time? Step back and ask yourself, "Whose agenda am I working on?"

You see, it's really a question of involvement. And as with Mary, it's not that God is indifferent to the fact we're running out of wine. But it is that we're trying to solve a situation that God knows more perfectly than we will ever know. His timing is divine; his timing is perfect. We're not going to move him along any faster than he determines.

Can we hurry God along? Remember, the process of making good wine is a *long* process. There are no shortcuts. Unless, of course, you are God.

❦

We're trying to solve a situation that God knows more perfectly than we will ever know.

❦

Prayer

God, so often I want to move things along at my pace. Why am I so reluctant to wait for your leading, your prompting? Help me, Lord, to be patient. Help me to make your timetable my timetable. Help me to trust you enough that I am able to sit and wait on you — no matter how hard that may be. Help me to see beyond my selfish demands, to your perfect will. I want to trust you God for all things. Give me the strength to wait upon you. Amen.

Talking Points

1. Why is patience such a difficult lesson for us to learn?

2. When we learn to wait on God, many times he teaches us more than just patience. He teaches us such things as trust and reliance. What else might God be trying to teach us?

6

WHO IS RESPONSIBLE
FOR MY SPIRITUAL CONDITION?
The Question of Will

Some time later, Jesus went up to Jerusalem for a feast of the Jews. Now there is in Jerusalem near the Sheep Gate a pool, which in Aramaic is called Bethesda and which is surrounded by five covered colonnades. Here a great number of disabled people used to lie – the blind, the lame, the paralyzed. One who was there had been an invalid for thirty-eight years. When Jesus saw him lying there and learned that he had been in this condition for a long time, he asked him, **"Do you want to get well?"**

"Sir," the invalid replied, "I have no one to help me into the pool when the water is stirred. While I am trying to get in, someone else goes down ahead of me."

Then Jesus said to him, "Get up! Pick up your mat and walk." At once the man was cured; he picked up his mat and walked.

The day on which this took place was a Sabbath, and so the Jews said to the man who had been healed, "It is the Sabbath; the law forbids you to carry your mat."

But he replied, "The man who made me well said to me, 'Pick up your mat and walk.'" So they asked him, "Who is this fellow who told you to pick it up and walk?" The man who was healed had no idea who it was, for Jesus had slipped away into the crowd that was there.

Later Jesus found him at the temple and said to him, "See, you are well again. Stop sinning or something worse may happen to you."

~John 5:1-14[36]

"Do you want to get well?" It seems like a strange question to ask someone who's not well!

"Do you want to get well?" If you didn't know that Jesus asked the question, you might think it was rhetorical. For as we've already suggested *Jesus never asked a question because he needed to know the answer.*

He didn't ask this question simply to gather information or secure facts. No, Jesus divinely designed his question to emphasize inward change. Jesus asked the question for the benefit of the invalid who'd sat there for so very long.

But as straightforward as the question is, the answer Jesus gets is anything but direct. The invalid says neither "Yes," nor "No."

While in Israel during college, I occasionally enjoyed jogging around the walls of the Old City of Jerusalem, in and out of the various gates. At first, every gate looked like the next and I got lost easily. But I soon learned to recognize each gate and remember its unique place in the history of the city.

Most of Jerusalem's gates have several names signifying their principle function or location. For example: the Water Gate, the Horse Gate, the East Gate, the Fountain Gate, the Valley Gate, the Golden Gate, Herod's Gate, Lion's Gate, Damascus Gate, the Inspection Gate, the Fish Gate, Zion Gate, the New Gate, and my personal favorite, the Dung Gate![37]

But one gate in particular takes center stage in our story. It was through the Sheep Gate that worshippers brought sheep into the temple area for sacrifice. Constructed when Nehemiah rebuilt the walls of Jerusalem about 445 B.C.[38] it survived some 500 years before Jesus walked through it.

Located just inside the Sheep Gate, tradition tells us the pool where this invalid lay had been used to wash the sheep before they were sacrificed. Luke tells us that pool – called Bethesda – was a popular place, particularly for disabled people: *"the blind, the lame, the paralyzed."* Here they would have sat in the shade provided by a roof held up by colonnades.

Among these sufferers sat a man who'd been an invalid for thirty-eight years. This doesn't mean he sat by the pool day and night for thirty-eight years. He may have known someone who brought him there from time to time, perhaps even daily. Possibly he actually did live there, but we can't be certain.

HOUSE OF KINDNESS

When Jesus saw him lying there and learned that he'd been in this condition for a long time, he asked him, ***"Do you want to get well?"***

Imagine the scene that day. A pool surrounded by the helpless, hopeless, and lifeless. The smell of sheep in the air.

And Jesus. Standing there, perhaps with his hand stretched out, his eyes fixed on *this singular figure.* And he asks, ***"Do you want to get well?"***

And so, not because Jesus needed to know, but rather for the sake of the invalid, he asks the question, ***"Do you want to get well?"***

"Sir," the invalid replied, "I have no one to help me into the pool when the water is stirred. While I am trying to get in, someone else goes down ahead of me."

The invalid fooled himself into believing he wanted to get in the pool. He sat there so long, he forgot why he'd sat there in the first place.

Are you this man, full of excuses why this or that gets in the way?

But Jesus has a way of looking beyond the façade, beyond the rationalizations. He looks beyond the *excuses. With Jesus, we never have to wonder whether the correct question is being asked.* Every question is the right question for the right time. Jesus did not ask the invalid if he wanted to be healed because the man approached *him* or showed some evidence of faith. After all, the man sat there four decades!

And Jesus meets us where we are. He knows where you are today. He knows what's on your mind. He knows what you're thinking. He knows what is preoccupying your thoughts. He knows you're struggling with lust. He knows you're discouraged. He knows the love you once had for your spouse is not there anymore. He knows you've given up on a solution. In fact, there really isn't much difference between you and the invalid.

Are you this man, lying around for years, full of excuses as to why *this* or *that* gets in the way? Have you wasted your whole life waiting for something that never comes?

And like the invalid's answer to Jesus' question, why is it when God asks us something, often we give him an indirect answer?

You're sitting at the pool of Bethesda. And actually, it's really not that bad. You've gotten quite comfortable. *You may even think you're better off sitting there.*

Notice that *faith* is never mentioned in this passage. Did the invalid have faith? While God is pleased to see our faith, he does not need it to show his glory. God is still the God of miracles. While he doesn't always choose to do so, he can heal. And so with the words, "Get up! Pick up your mat and walk ..." Jesus reaches out in grace and heals the man.

Instantly cured, he obeys Jesus. He picks up his mat and walks. I would love to have been there that day when a man who'd been lying on a bed for thirty-eight years suddenly got up and walked away!

GRADUATION DAY

On a sultry June evening some three decades ago, I watched the commencement ceremony of the Central Columbia High School graduating class of 1983. The graduation took place in a university auditorium that held several thousand. Arriving a little late and aware there weren't any seats left on the main floor, I sat in the balcony.

It was a particularly *moving* experience for me because it was my sister-in-law's brother, Scott, graduating that night from high school. After 21 years of schooling, the school district decided to graduate Scott because he was too old to continue to attend.

You see, Scott has Down syndrome.

I'll never forget the moment they read Scott's name. He slowly ascended the stairs to the platform. In that large auditorium, I thought I actually heard his shoes shuffling across the stage. Here was a kid who was undoubtedly the butt of many a joke in the halls of high school. Students can be cruel, even if you are not mentally or physically challenged.

But commencement exercises have a way of bringing out the best in everyone. And as Scott took his diploma, he did something no other student did that entire evening. He put his arms up, held them proudly in the air above his head, and walked in his slow, deliberate pace across the stage.

And the whole place lost it. Everyone in Scott's graduating class rose to their feet and gave him a standing ovation to thunderous applause.

His sister, my sister-in-law, waited on the other side to help him down the stairs.

I wonder how many of us will someday walk across that platform in heaven as we receive the crowns of Christ. I wonder how many of us will graduate from habits and secret sins that debilitate us spiritually. And I can't help but envision the crowd of saints who've gone before us rising to their feet as we shed the sin nature for good, and see for the first time with our eyes our Lord and Savior Jesus Christ. What a day that will be!

Don't lose sight of the fact that the invalid was healed *before* he got up. How many of us see God move in our lives, yet still remain paralyzed by our unbelief?

SITTING BY BETHESDA

Perhaps you have been hurt by a colleague or friend, or spouse or former spouse. Perhaps by God. And you've been sitting by Bethesda. You're not able to get up. On the outside you want to get up, but on the inside you have some reason that prevents you. You've been sitting by the pool avoiding the issue, avoiding the question. You lack the motivation. You lack the strength. You lack the faith to believe that God can do anything with you.

Jesus wants to know, **"Do you want to get well?"**

⊙☙⊙

Jesus asks you, "Do you want to get well?"

⊙☙⊙

Maybe you, like the invalid, have sat there for so long you actually enjoy the comfort that sitting there provides. *It's been so long since you originally sat down, you've forgotten why you sat there in the first place.*

Jesus asks you, **"Do you want to get well?" "Do you want to get well?"**

It's easy to sit by the pool and come up with reasons why we can't move. We can even fool ourselves, like the invalid, into believing we really want to get in the pool! **"Do you want to get well?"** Are you lying around blaming someone else for your spiritual health?

⊙☙⊙

Are you sitting by Bethesda? "Do you want to get well?"

⊙☙⊙

Are you lying around wishing for a better prayer life? Are you sitting around waiting for someone to help you read your Bible? Are you waiting to get to *know* him better? Are you sitting around waiting for the waters to be stirred? It's not going to happen. Are you sitting by Bethesda?

"Do you want to get well?" Spiritual apathy is our choice. Who is responsible for my spiritual condition? We have no one to blame but ourselves.

In case you didn't notice, the man never did get into the pool.[39] He waited thirty-eight years for something he wanted, never got, and in the end, didn't need. And when he was finally healed, he had no idea who healed him.

The invalid didn't need the pool to experience the water of life. He needed Jesus in his life. He needed a change of will and a determination that through Jesus' power and strength his life would be different.

Are you sitting by Bethesda? *"Do you want to get well?"*

Prayer

God, I confess I've been sitting by Bethesda for a long time. I'm waiting for something – anything – that will make me feel better. I have an answer for anyone who will dare ask. But you know it's just an excuse. Help me to see Lord, you are standing there with your hand stretched out – your eyes are fixed on me – no one else, and you're asking me, "Do you want to get well? ... Do you really want to get well?" Give me the faith to stand up, Lord. Give me the faith that has long since escaped my grasp. Help me, Lord, to pick up my bed and walk. Amen.

Talking Points

1. Excuses, excuses; we all have them. Why is it easier to make an excuse for why we don't want to do something, than to actually do it?

2. Jesus warns the invalid to stop sinning "or something worse may happen." What would you say to that kind of warning?

"Judge a person by their questions,
rather than their answers."
Voltaire

Part III:
Growing Stronger

7

HOW CAN I FIND LASTING PEACE?
The Question of Forgiveness

Now one of the Pharisees invited Jesus to have dinner with him, so he went to the Pharisee's house and reclined at the table. When a woman who had lived a sinful life in that town learned that Jesus was eating at the Pharisee's house, she brought an alabaster jar of perfume, and as she stood behind him at his feet weeping, she began to wet his feet with her tears. Then she wiped them with her hair, kissed them and poured perfume on them.

When the Pharisee who had invited him saw this, he said to himself, "If this man were a prophet, he would know who is touching him and what kind of woman she is – that she is a sinner."

Jesus answered him, "Simon, I have something to tell you."

"Tell me, teacher," he said.

"Two men owed money to a certain moneylender. One owed him five hundred denarii, and the other fifty. Neither of them had the money to pay him back, so he canceled the debts of both. **Now which of them will love him more?"**

Simon replied, "I suppose the one who had the bigger debt canceled."

"You have judged correctly," Jesus said. Then he turned toward the woman and said to Simon,

"Do you see this woman?"

~Luke 7:36-44

You and I don't know this woman, but apparently she was notorious. Luke says she lived a sinful life in that town. He doesn't tell us her name or the nature of her sin. Whatever her sin, the kind of life she lived was no secret. Everyone in town knew about her, including Simon the Pharisee.

That Jesus knew her, and that she knew Jesus is also clear. Scripture doesn't tell us when, but on some other occasion this woman met Jesus and experienced forgiveness for her sins. Perhaps she had talked with him many times before. How do we know? Because she brought an alabaster jar of perfume to anoint him.

On *this* occasion, Luke records, she returns to thank him by wiping the dust off his feet. Her reputation, though, was not so easily wiped away.

ᐸᕼᐁᕼᐳ

Jesus knows the innermost thoughts of Pharisees.

ᐸᕼᐁᕼᐳ

She stands behind Jesus weeping, her tears falling on his feet. Caught up in the moment, she crosses all social boundaries, and lets her hair down in public to wipe his feet. And *that* infuriates Simon the Pharisee! *"If this man were a prophet, he would know who is touching him."*

Simon didn't say these things aloud; he merely thinks them. *But Jesus knows the innermost thoughts of Pharisees.* He knows what we're thinking to ourselves when that co-worker gets the promotion that we should have gotten. He knows what we're thinking when we roll our eyes at the parent whose kid is throwing a tantrum in the middle of Target. He knows what we're thinking when we can't take our eyes off that woman in her low-cut dress. He knows what we're thinking when we nudge our friend as a teenager walks by with an earring in his nose or his eyebrow or his tongue. *He knows the innermost thoughts of such as we.*

"Simon, I have something to tell you," Jesus says. Our attention turns to a conversation between Jesus and Simon. In contemporary terms the story goes like this: two men run up their charge cards.

One owed ten times as much as the other. Both were unable to meet the minimum monthly payment, and in an act of pure grace and mercy, the lending institution forgave both their debts.

And then Jesus says to Simon, *"Now which of them will love him more? Do you see this woman?"*

Jesus asks Simon two *seemingly* unrelated questions. Whenever Jesus asks two or more questions in a series, they are identical in purpose. That is to say, Jesus seeks *one* response, yet he may ask more than one question to bring someone to that single understanding. *"Now which of them will love him more?" "Do you see this woman?"* Jesus asks Simon these two questions to show him that he knows what kind of woman is touching him.

It seems like a strange question to ask someone who's bent out of shape over what the woman is doing. This second question is an understatement – *"Do you see this woman?"*

That's all Simon sees! Simon doesn't see anything but the sinner who is all over Jesus. A sinner touching Jesus!

BLINDED BY SIN

Sometimes a person can be so possessed by their own thoughts and motives that they are blinded by prejudice and envy and hatred and lust and greed.

When Moses – angered by the complaining Israelites – struck the rock, you can be sure Moses only saw their sin.[40]

When God asked Jonah to go to Nineveh to preach, Jonah couldn't get past the reputation of the Ninevites.[41]

When Cain killed his brother Abel, he couldn't get past his own anger, jealousy, and pride.[42]

When Joseph's ten brothers sold him into slavery in Egypt because his father loved him more and gave him a coat of many colors – they couldn't get past their jealousy of him.[43]

So when Jesus asks Simon, *"Do you see this woman?"* you can be sure the woman is all that Simon saw. Do you get the picture?

Simon has his eyes on the woman, the woman has her eyes on Jesus, and Jesus has his eyes on Simon.

Why does Jesus ask, **"Do you see this woman?"** if Simon is already looking at the woman? *Why does Jesus ask him if he sees her?*

Jesus doesn't ask Simon the question so Simon can compare himself to the woman and feel good about himself; Simon was already doing that! No, Jesus asks Simon the question because there is something about the woman Simon needs to see. Simon needs to see that the woman knows she is forgiven – something Simon has not experienced.

The older brother of the prodigal son could have been asked the same thing: "Do you see your brother?" When the younger brother returned from throwing away the inheritance his father had given him, the older brother stayed out in the field as the whole household celebrated the return of the prodigal son. Why? Because the older brother couldn't get past his own resentment. The older brother needed to see what the prodigal brother had seen and experienced: the forgiveness of his father.

Cain needed to see beyond his own pride to the forgiveness God offered.

Joseph's brothers needed to see beyond their jealousy to the blessings that were already theirs through the Abrahamic Covenant confirmed to their own father, Jacob, whom God later renamed Israel.

ೞ✥ೞ

Whenever we look judgmentally at someone to make ourselves feel better, we've become like Simon the Pharisee.

ೞ✥ೞ

And in the same way, some of us – like Simon – need to stop comparing ourselves to others in order to make ourselves feel better. What we need is what this woman had: an experience of God's forgiveness.

It wasn't that Simon didn't need forgiveness from sins. He just didn't see himself as having any sins to be forgiven.

Whenever we look judgmentally at someone to make ourselves feel better, we've become like Simon the Pharisee.[44] Jesus asks us, **"Do you see this woman?"** not so we can feel good about ourselves, but so we realize pride is blinding us from experiencing God's forgiveness. *Jesus wants to move our focus from the sin to the forgiveness.*

CHAIRMAN OF THE BOARD

A few years ago we began attending a new church. We chose to worship at the Saturday night service. We often saw the same gentleman back in the nursery wing of the church coming out of the janitor's room. Not until I saw an announcement in the church bulletin stating he would speak on Sunday morning, did I discover his true identity. The janitor bringing the morning message was the chairman of the elder board. *All I had seen was a janitor.*

Jesus is *not* asking, 'What do you see when you see this woman?' He's saying, 'Look beyond what you see on the outside – to the heart within. *He's asking Simon if he sees more than meets the eye.*

Can you see more than meets the eye? Can you see this woman's good deed as a display of her gratefulness? Do you think she understands the depth at which she has been forgiven?

All Simon sees is a sinner touching Jesus and he thinks Jesus hasn't got a clue! To Simon, the woman's life was a failure. The sin in her life marked her so that she was useless and of no value to anyone. She was something to be discarded.

But not so with Jesus. Not so with Luke. As I said at the beginning of this chapter, Luke doesn't mention what kind of "sinner" the woman was. *Perhaps it was because Luke did not see her as a sinner anymore.*

Overwhelmed with emotion, the woman doesn't care that everyone is watching. She doesn't care that Simon is upset. She has been forgiven. *All she cares about is Jesus.* Her tears are not tears of repentance. They are tears of joy, tears of gratitude, tears of forgiveness, tears of peace.

And so for the benefit of those who are listening, Jesus says, *"Your sins are forgiven."* He didn't need to tell the woman – she already knew her sins were forgiven. No, Jesus said it for the benefit of those, like Simon, who were sitting there that day.

ᏮᏋᎧᏋ

What you do for Jesus shows you understand his forgiveness.

ᏮᏋᎧᏋ

In case you didn't notice, this woman never spoke a word. She displayed her love for Jesus in her gratefulness. What she does for Jesus shows she understands what it means to be forgiven. It is something she set out to do as an expression of her love for Jesus. What you *do* for Jesus shows you understand his forgiveness.

And as she stood behind him at his feet weeping, she began to wet his feet with her tears. Then she wiped them with her hair, kissed them and poured perfume on them.

How can you find lasting peace? Lasting peace comes from knowing you are forgiven. Do you know the lasting peace of gratitude? *Do you know the lasting peace of forgiveness?* Do *you* see this woman?

Prayer

Forgive me Lord, for those times when I become like Simon, and lose my focus of the real issue. I thank you for the complete forgiveness that is mine in Jesus Christ. I love you Lord, and sometimes I'm too embarrassed or caught up in myself to show it. Thank you for the example of this woman who wasn't afraid to turn her love into action. Amen.

Talking Points

1. Do you agree with the statement 'forgiveness is a choice not a feeling?'

2. Why is it that we experience peace when we know we are forgiven?

3. Moses, Jonah, Cain, and Joseph's ten brothers are just a few of those who could not get beyond their own anger, jealousy or pride. Can you think of any other Bible characters that were blinded by sin?

8

WHY DOESN'T GOD ANSWER MY PRAYERS EXACTLY AS I PRAY?
The Question of Prerogative

A few days later, when Jesus again entered Capernaum, the people heard that he had come home. So many gathered that there was no room left, not even outside the door, and he preached the word to them. Some men came, bringing to him a paralytic, carried by four of them. Since they could not get him to Jesus because of the crowd, they made an opening in the roof above Jesus and, after digging through it, lowered the mat the paralyzed man was lying on. When Jesus saw their faith, he said to the paralytic, "Son, your sins are forgiven."

Now some teachers of the law were sitting there, thinking to themselves, "Why does this fellow talk like that? He's blaspheming! Who can forgive sins but God alone?"

Immediately Jesus knew in his spirit that this was what they were thinking in their hearts, and he said to them, **"Why are you thinking these things? Which is easier: to say to the paralytic, 'Your sins are forgiven,' or to say, 'Get up, take your mat and walk'? But** *that you may know that the Son of Man has authority to forgive sins..." He said to the paralytic, "I tell you, get up, take up your mat and go home."*

He got up, took his mat and walked out in full view of them all. This amazed everyone and they praised God, saying,

"We have never seen anything like this!"

~Mark 2:1-11

Had I witnessed this miracle I would have rated it high for dramatic effect and flashiness! The ceiling opens up, mud and debris fall everywhere, sunlight streams in on the perplexed crowd. And suddenly through the dust, a paralytic is lowered on a stretcher cutting Jesus' lesson short.

Mark doesn't even attempt to tell us *what* Jesus is teaching. It's not important. All eyes focus on the ceiling, like all eyes focus on a bride as she makes her grand entrance from the back of a church. I would guess, however, Jesus looks not up, but rather on the hearts of those sitting around him. He looks past the clothes, the education, the position in life. He looks straight to the heart.

UP ON THE ROOF TOP

While in college, I spent a year studying in Israel. I lived at what is now called Jerusalem University College, located on Mt. Zion. More than once, I climbed on top of the Turkish walls encircling the Old City and enjoyed a view from high above the noise and bustle of the crowded streets and alleys. On occasion, I lounged on the college roof and listened to the music from a concert in the city park below the school.

For as far as I could see, there were only flat roofs – no gable or A-frame roofs. If you visit Israel, you will quickly see that all the homes and buildings are constructed of stone, marble, and bricks. My photos – taken from atop the walls looking down at these flat stone roofs – reveal how the residents hang their laundry out to dry, and store their drinking water in tanks.

Mark states, *"Since they could not get him to Jesus because of the crowd, they made an opening in the roof above..."* (The parallel passage to this miracle in Luke says the men tried to find a way to get the paralytic to Jesus and couldn't.)[45] So the radical way to Jesus in this situation was through the ceiling.

Sickness in the Bible many times is the result of disobedience to God's explicit commands.[46] And conversely, forgiveness was often demonstrated by healing.[47] *The roof, then, became the door to healing.*

But I can imagine there were probably those who saw this entrance from the roof as a great inconvenience. But not Jesus. *He's never interrupted by our timing or needs.*

I can also imagine the initial disappointment the four must have felt when all their effort was rewarded with, *"Son, your sins are forgiven."* They didn't bring the paralytic to Jesus to have his sins forgiven! *They had hoped for a miracle.*

Mark tells us that some teachers of the law sat there. Luke adds the description *Pharisees*.[48] So when Jesus said, *"Your sins are forgiven ... "* it's not what the teachers of the law expected to hear either. *"He's blaspheming!"* they said.

So why doesn't God answer our prayers exactly as we pray? If you read the Bible long enough, you'll discover very few of our *whys* are ever answered. *Why do I have breast cancer? Why did I lose my job? Why can't we have children?*

Jesus is never interrupted by our timing or needs.

Why is it we pray for something, only to find that God answers it some other way, entirely different from the way we prayed?

Some people think it shows maturity not to ask *why*. I don't think asking *why* says anything about maturity. It shows maturity *to ask* why and then stand securely in our faith when we don't receive the answer we are looking for. Maturity is found in what we *do* when we don't find an answer.

If you read the Bible long enough, you'll discover very few of our whys are ever answered.

But I don't accept the notion that *we can't know* the answer to our questions. For some of us it might be true. We'll never know the reason because we hear what God says yet won't accept it. We *can't* know the answer because we *won't* allow it.

For others, there are answers to be found. We learn them very quickly. I won't attempt to explain why God allows a child to die when we pray for his recovery or why we can pray for healing in a marriage, only to see it fall apart.

Prayers have a way of bringing us around to God's way of thinking. **"Which is easier: to say to the paralytic, 'Your sins are forgiven,' or to say, 'Get up, take your mat and walk'?"** This question, early in Jesus' ministry – looks at an event when someone came to Jesus looking for one answer – and received another.

For the paralytic, Jesus used the opportunity to show he was the Son of Man. He used the miracle to show he had the authority to forgive sins. Jesus' concern for the paralytic's spiritual condition took precedence over the man's physical condition.

Now some teachers of the law were sitting there, thinking to themselves, "Why does this fellow talk like that? He's blaspheming! Who can forgive sins but God alone?"

This was not something they discussed openly. These scribes were thinking these things in their hearts. And Jesus knew what they were thinking. Perhaps anyone could have been sharp enough to predict what the scribes and Pharisees were thinking. But Jesus did not guess – he immediately knew their thoughts in his spirit.

He answers their question (the one in their thoughts) with a question. Jesus does this many times in the Gospels. For example, when they asked Jesus, "Is it right to pay taxes to Caesar?" *"Whose portrait is on this coin?"* he asked in return.

Or after the rich young ruler asked, "Good teacher, what must I do to inherit eternal life?" he returned, *"Why do you call me good?"*

So, here in the room with the forgiven paralytic, Jesus asks them why they are questioning these things. Without giving the teachers of the law a chance to answer, he presents them with a rhetorical question: **"Why are you thinking these things? Which is easier: to say to the paralytic, 'Your sins are forgiven,' or to say, 'Get up, take your mat and walk'?"**

Which *is* easier to say? 'Your sins are forgiven' or 'take up your mat and walk'? As far as saying either – neither presents more difficultly in pronunciation than the other. But if you're sitting in a crowded room of people (as Jesus was) all intently listening to every word that drops from your lips, *which is easier to say?*

'*Your sins are forgiven,*' is easier *to say* – no one can *see* whether Jesus forgives the sins. But if I say to you, 'take up your mat and walk' – I'd better have what it takes to get you up on your feet!

So while saying, '*Your sins are forgiven,*' is easier *to say*, it's not easier to *do*. Forgiving sins took his death to accomplish. We don't have to give our life to forgive someone (like Jesus did); yet, it sometimes is more difficult to forgive someone who has wronged us. How easy is it for you to forgive someone who has wronged you? We all know too well it is a lot easier to *say* we forgive someone than actually *do* it.

Mark tells us '*Jesus saw their faith ...*' Can others *see* your faith? How far out of the way are you willing to go to bring your friends to Jesus? (Climb on a roof?) Can others see by what you do that you have great faith?

Why doesn't God answer my prayers exactly as I pray? *Because he is in control.* Not you. Not me. We pray for *healing* and *he forgives sins!* Jesus knows exactly what we need when we pray. But if you read the rest of the story, he does heal the paralytic. *That's his prerogative.*

But there's also another reason. Jesus addresses our needs, not just our desires.

Jesus says, *"But that you may know that the Son of Man has authority to forgive sins...I tell you, get up, take up your mat and go home."* In other words, "I'm going to validate what I say, with a miracle: you're healed. Get up and you can go home. And take your mat with you, so those who see you will know, and see you have been healed." To say it yet another

⊙⟨⟩⊙

Can others see by what you do that you have great faith? Can others see by what you do that you have great faith?

⊙⟨⟩⊙

way: "In order that you may know I can do *that* (that is, forgive sins), I'll do *this* (heal)."

Jesus knows something about faith: the eye of faith can see forgiveness; the blind eye of the Pharisees can only see walking.

He got up, took his mat and walked out in full view of them all. This amazed everyone and they praised God, saying, "We have never seen anything like this!"

And the crippled stands up. Imagine if he had not obeyed. Jesus' visual object lesson would have fallen flat on its face! Those sitting there knew this man's sins were forgiven immediately because he was healed immediately. To him, the miracle meant a cleansed life and a new opportunity. Obedience brings blessing to others and glory to God.

Why doesn't God answer my prayers exactly as I pray?

If Jesus healed only the man's physical condition, he would have walked away never experiencing the forgiveness of God. Some of us have fooled ourselves into believing our life here on earth has everything to do with our physical well-being, when in reality our life on earth has everything to do with our spiritual well-being.

Why doesn't God answer my prayers exactly as I pray? Because he is God, and I am not. Because he is in control. *That's his prerogative.*

Prayer

Father, often times I – like the paralytic – come to you asking for one thing, only to have you answer my prayers in an unexpected way. I ask for healing, and you say, "Your sins are forgiven." It's not what I want, but now I realize it's exactly what I need. Help me to approach all of my requests with an open heart and mind which allows for the possibility that the answer I receive is the perfect reply of a perfect God. Amen.

Talking Points

1. Sometimes people approach God with the attitude, "God, if you only listen to me this one time, I promise I'll never bother you again." What's wrong with this kind of approach to God?

2. Can you recall a time when you asked God for one thing and he answered with something unexpected? As you look back now, is it clear to you why God chose to answer in the way he did?

9

HOW MUCH DO I LOVE HIM?
The Question of Devotion

Afterward Jesus appeared again to his disciples, by the Sea of Tiberias. It happened this way: Peter, Thomas ..., Nathanael, the sons of Zebedee, and two other disciples were together. "I'm going out to fish," Peter told them, and they said, "We'll go with you." So they went out and got into the boat, but that night they caught nothing. Early in the morning, Jesus stood on the shore, but the disciples did not realize that it was Jesus. He called out to them, **"Friends, haven't you any fish?"**

"No," they answered. He said, "Throw your net on the right side of the boat and you will find some." When they did, they were unable to haul the net in because of the large number of fish.

Then the disciple whom Jesus loved said to Peter, "It is the Lord!" As soon as Peter heard him say, "It is the Lord," he ... jumped into the water. The other disciples followed in the boat, towing the net full of fish .... When they landed, they saw a fire of burning coals there with fish on it, and some bread. Jesus said to them, "Bring some of the fish you have just caught."

Peter climbed aboard and dragged the net ashore. It was full of large fish, 153 ... Jesus said to them, "Come and have breakfast." This was now the third time Jesus appeared to his disciples after he was raised from the dead.

When they had finished eating, Jesus said to Peter, **"Simon son of John, do you truly love me more than these?"**

"Yes, Lord," he said, "you know that I love you."

Jesus said, "Feed my lambs."

Again Jesus said, **"Simon son of John, do you truly love me?"**
He answered, "Yes, Lord, you know that I love you."

Jesus said, "Take care of my sheep."

The third time he said to him, **"Simon son of John, do you love me?"**

Peter was hurt because Jesus asked him the third time, **"Do you love me?"** *He said, "Lord, you know all things; you know that I love you."*

Jesus said, "Feed my sheep."
~John 21:1-17

Sometime after his resurrection, but before his ascension, Jesus appeared to his disciples at the Sea of Galilee as recorded here by the Apostle John. The last days and weeks brought tremendous change into the lives of the disciples. Their leader, Jesus, talked of "going up to Jerusalem" to die. And that was what, in fact, had happened. They hadn't really understood the full impact of what Jesus was talking about at the time. They were confused. They were baffled by the occurrences and events of the last month. And I'm not so sure the time between Jesus' death and this event helped their understanding.

I can't help but wonder what was going through Peter's mind that morning.

During the short time Jesus spent with his disciples in the Upper Room, Jesus told Peter he would deny him. *"Will you really lay down your life for me? I tell you the truth, before the rooster crows, you will disown me three times!"*[49] Peter reacted strongly at the suggestion he would deny his master! But sadly, those words are fulfilled only a few, short hours later. *As Simon Peter stood warming himself, he was asked, "You are not one of the disciples, are you?" He denied it, saying, "I am not." One of the high priest's servants, a relative of the man whose ear Peter had cut off, challenged him, "Didn't I see you with him in the olive grove?" Again Peter denied it, and at that moment a rooster began to crow.*[50]

When we come to the passage in John 21, we must keep in mind that hanging over Peter's head were the words of denial he spoke against the one with whom he'd just devoted three years of his *life. It's not hard to understand what Peter was feeling here, when he announced, "I'm going out to fish."*

After Jesus' death, Peter returns to the one thing he knows best: fishing! Jesus was gone – out of sight, out of mind. Nothing left to do but fish. Business as usual!

So it's early in the morning when a stranger on the shore asks the disciples if they've caught any fish. They answer "No," and he tells them where to throw their nets. They soon realize it is Jesus and they sit down to breakfast with him around a fire he has built.

When they finished eating, Jesus said to Simon Peter, **"Simon son of John, do you truly love me more than these?"**

I can picture the disciples sitting around the fire eating with our Lord ... they are hanging on every word he says; I mean, if they weren't paying attention before, they were certainly paying attention now.

I wonder if Peter looked into the flames of the fire and thought back to the moment when he stood around the fire with the servants and officials when he denied Jesus just days before.

And Jesus wants no one to misunderstand what he is about to say, so he says, **"Simon son of John ..."** Ninety-six times in the Gospels Simon Peter is simply called *"Peter."* Fifty times he is called *"Simon."* Twenty times he's known as *"Simon Peter."* Yet only five times is Peter called *"Simon son of John."* And three of those are right here in this passage.

When I was growing up, my mother would call me by my full name whenever she meant business. *"Christopher David Bozung!"* And it's no different here. So there's no question to whom Jesus is speaking, Jesus says, **"Simon son of John ... Do you truly love me? Do you truly love me more than these?"**

One of the reasons I enjoy this passage so much is because we have no idea to what ***these*** refers to.

HIGH SCHOOL ENGLISH

When I was in high school English, I learned you can't have a pronoun unless you have an antecedent. "Dick saw *Jane* run," becomes, "Dick saw *her* run." Here, however, there's no antecedent for the word "*these.*" We have a plural pronoun (*these*) referring to a *pronoun or noun* that doesn't exist in the Greek.

Many times, however, the antecedent is unspoken because the context dictates the subject of the conversation. If we're standing in a paint store and I say, "Do you see *anything?*" the context lets us both know we're talking about which *color* we'd like to choose.

In this case, the antecedent was understood by both Jesus and Peter, and John too, so John didn't feel the need to record it. Unfortunately for us, the question is ambiguous.

So what is Jesus referring to here? To what does the pronoun "these" refer? Perhaps Jesus was saying, *"Do you love me more than these other disciples love me?"* In other words, "How great is your love for me, Peter? Do you love me more than these other disciples love me?"

Or perhaps Jesus was referring to the other disciples. In other words, *"Do you love me more than you love these other disciples?"* Now Peter certainly was fond of the other disciples.

"Where is your devotion?" Jesus was asking him. *"You took my disciples away from what I had given them to do. Where is your heart? Is it with them or is it with me?"*

Maybe the "these" refers to something else ...

OUR FAVORITE PASTIME

Our family has been attending a Bible conference in Maryland for twenty-five years. My wife, Johnna, and I have been going for almost fifteen of those years. But we've been bringing our children for nine or ten years. And every year, one of the highlights of our stay at Sandy Cove is fishing off the dock. We started out with one pole. My two oldest children shared it. We actually talked my father into buying it by telling him he should buy his grandson's first fishing pole! And we did the same thing with the other two – and will probably do the same with the youngest who is not old enough to fish yet.

Last year we went out and bought a tackle box with all kinds of neat hooks and spinners. We even bought another pole and reel. And every year, right before we start down Highway 272 leading to the entrance of Sandy Cove, we stop and buy a box of night crawlers.

"Do you love me more than these?"

I guess you could say we love fishing. For us it's a pastime while we are at Sandy Cove.

Maybe the pronoun "*these*" refers to the fish. That would seem like a logical answer. After all, how many fish are there? Verse eleven tells us there were 153 fish. It would have been important for the disciples to count the fish in order to divide them among the seven disciples. But why does John feel *that* detail is important enough to tell *us*?

I can just see Peter sitting there in the middle of all those fish, counting: 71...72...73...74...151...152...153. He gets all done, and he's engrossed in the moment. And Jesus says to him, **"Simon Son of John, do you love me more than these?** Do you love me more than what these fish represent? Do you love me more than these?"

We know someone counted the fish. John doesn't tell us who – just that there were 153. Perhaps Peter, not knowing what to add to the breakfast conversation, sat silently counting the fish.

"Simon Son of John, do you love me more than these?" Do you love me more than fishing? Do you love me more than this occupation you've gone back to? How much do you love me, Peter? Enough to give up fishing once and for all and be true to me?

It is a natural reaction for us to say, "I'm hanging it up and going back to fishing." And that's the reason for Jesus' question to Peter.

Jesus has a higher calling for Peter than just fishing. "Follow me," Jesus told his disciples, "and I will make you fishers of men."[51]

It is a natural reaction for us to say, "I'm hanging it up and going back to fishing."

Jesus is asking this question, not for his own sake, but for the benefit of Peter. He knows where Peter's heart is. He wants Peter to know where Peter's heart is. "Peter, you've gone back to fishing ... where's your heart? Do you love me more than you love these?" (whether it is the fish, the other disciples, or *whatever*).

What is the "these" in your life? What is standing in the way of your devotion to Jesus?

How deep does your devotion go? How deep is your commitment to follow him when the walls fall in around you? Perhaps like Peter, you became disenchanted after being hurt. Perhaps you've gone through a divorce or lost someone close to you. Have you – like Peter – gone back to fishing *spiritually* speaking? How deep is your love for him?

I don't think it is an accident that the Greek is ambiguous. I believe it is by divine design. Perhaps God did not want us to know to *what* or *whom* Jesus was referring, because he asks us the same question: **"Do you truly love me more than these?"**

What is the "*these*" in your life? What is standing in the way of your devotion to Jesus? What is it that Jesus asks you to make a choice between? How would you answer the question Jesus asks: **"Do you love me more than these?"** What are the *these* in your life?

Prayer

Oh, I love you Lord, but may you help me realize there may be something or someone standing in the way. Help me to examine my own heart, "Do I love you more than these, Lord?" Like Peter, I've gone back to fishing spiritually speaking. I pray you will give me the strength through your Holy Spirit to turn back to you. You never called Peter just to fish ... you never called me just to fish. Help me to see you have a higher calling in my life than just fishing. Amen.

Talking Points

1. This question of Jesus has the capacity to touch every area of our life. The question is also highly personal. Is there something in your life right now that is standing in the way of your devotion to God?

2. When things get tough, it is easy for us to echo the words of Peter, "I'm going back to fishing." Why do we feel that way?

"You can tell whether a man is clever by his answers. You can tell whether a man is wise by his questions."
Naguib Mahfouz

Part IV:
In Time of Testing

10

DOES GOD REALLY CARE?
The Question of Trust

That day when evening came, he said to his disciples, "Let us go over to the other side." Leaving the crowd behind, they took him along, just as he was, in the boat. There were also other boats with him. A furious squall came up, and the waves broke over the boat, so that it was nearly swamped. Jesus was in the stern, sleeping on a cushion. The disciples woke him and said to him, "Teacher, don't you care if we drown?"

He got up, rebuked the wind and said to the waves, "Quiet! Be still!" Then the wind died down and it was completely calm.

*He said to his disciples, **"Why are you so afraid? Do you still have no faith?"***

They were terrified and asked each other, "Who is this? Even the wind and the waves obey him!"

~Mark 4:35-41

A wild sea and a furious storm. A ship out of control and a fearful crew. *In the midst of the violence, a sleeping passenger with the power to make it all go away.*

Mark's description of Jesus asleep on the Sea of Galilee mirrors the description of Jonah asleep in the belly of a ship centuries earlier.

A WHALE OF A STORY

I doubt in the moment of crisis that the disciples' thoughts flashed back to Jonah's ship bound for Tarshish. But the parallels are strong. When the sailors in *that* boat could stand it no longer, they woke Jonah who was in a deep sleep. And when they threw him in the sea, the storm ceased. When the Twelve could stand it no longer, they woke Jesus. And he calmed the sea. Jonah *had a choice* to stop the raging storm, and so did Jesus.

The four Gospel writers record Jesus getting into, getting out of, or teaching from a boat more than twenty times. Traveling by boat was not only the most common mode of transportation in the Galilee region, but the quickest way to a city on the other side. Yet however common as traveling by boat was, this was an uncommon voyage. This time Jesus sleeps in the stern of the boat.

And he uses the great sea, the raging storm, and his sound sleep to test the disciples' faith and teach about his deity.

The miracle that Mark writes about is known to many as the "Stilling of the Storm." It takes place in the evening after Jesus spent the day teaching. He and the disciples went across the Sea of Galilee without the crowd.

I imagine that tired after a long day of teaching, Jesus laid his head down shortly after giving the command to the disciples to go to the other side. I imagine he had neither time to change his clothes nor time to get something to eat.

So there was a very practical reason for crossing over to the other side. Jesus is exhausted. And he's ready to take a much-needed break.

WANNA WATCH A MOVIE?

Several months ago, our family had a stretch of hectic weeks. So we decided to go for a bike ride to a park where we played a while. From there we peddled to Burger King, ate lunch, rode to an ice cream store, and then walked around downtown before biking home. We earlier rented a family DVD, so we moved the coffee table out of the way in the living room, made popcorn, and watched the movie.

We needed to come away from the busyness of the world – ministry in particular. Coming away by ourselves for a while gave us the rest and proper perspective that we needed.

Jesus knew the importance of taking time away for himself. The demands of ministry, the pressing needs of the people, the constant attacks of the religious leaders – all these drained his energy. Fatigue had set in, and Jesus needed to get away.

But don't fool yourself into thinking that sleep is the only thing on Jesus' mind.

Their journey across the lake placed Jesus and the disciples in the middle of the sea, and set the stage for a lesson on faith. With Jesus lying in the stern of the boat on a cushion, the disciples make their way to the middle of the sea. Then Mark tells us, *"A furious squall came up, and the waves broke over the boat, so that it was nearly swamped."*

And the disciples trembled with fear.

Many of the disciples were seasoned fishermen and should have been accustomed to storms on the sea. Evidently this tempest was more than they were used to. Mark describes the storm as a "fierce gale of wind" with "waves breaking over the boat so much so that the boat was already filling up."

Adding to the disciples' anxiety, they discover Jesus sleeping. And this, too, contributes to their fear. How can Jesus sleep at a time like this? It's similar to what some people feel when they experience a frightening storm in

ⓒⓔⓢⓞ

It's a small step from there to pointing our finger at God. "Where is God? Is he unaware?"

ⓒⓔⓢⓞ

their life – loss of employment, loss of a relationship, loss of a loved one. Fear. Loneliness. Anxiety. Hopelessness. And it's a small step from there to pointing our finger at God. In such despair it's easy for us to wonder, "Where is God? Is he unaware?" It's too easy for us – like the disciples – to accuse Jesus of not caring.

This miracle displays the divine side of Jesus, but highlights his human side as well. We tend to see Jesus like his portrayal in a medieval painting: a flat portrait with a circle of light around his head. We don't often think of Jesus as someone who needed to sleep or who showed human emotions ... but he did! Jesus cried at the grave of his friend Lazarus.[52] Jesus wept over the city of Jerusalem.[53] Jesus, when he was in the Garden of Gethsemane, said to his disciples, *"My soul is overwhelmed with sorrow to the point of death ..."*[54] The writer to the Hebrews said of Jesus: *"We do not have a high priest who is unable to sympathize with our weaknesses, but we have one who has been tempted in every way, just as we are – yet without sin. Let us then approach the throne of grace with confidence, so that we may receive mercy and find grace to help us in our time of need."*[55]

So when I'm tempted to think Jesus doesn't understand what I am feeling, I take comfort in the fact that Scripture records that he cried too. And on occasion, he was exhausted.

It's easy for me to think God doesn't care how I feel. It's easy for me to think he's unaware of what I am going through. It's easy for me to think he's not *there. When there is more water on the inside of the boat than outside the boat, it's too easy to see him as asleep in our lives.*

ⓖⲈⲐⲐⲒ

God can and will use the circumstances of life to build our faith in him.

ⓖⲈⲐⲐⲒ

God uses the circumstances of life to teach us who he is. God uses the circumstances of life to teach us who we are. God uses the circumstances of life to build our faith in him.

What did Jesus do? Mark tells us, *"He got up, rebuked the wind and said to the wave, 'Quiet! Be still!' Then the wind died, down and it was completely calm."*

He said to his disciples, **"Why are you so afraid? Do you still have no faith?"**

Notice that the disciples were more afraid after the storm than during it. Mark tells us, *"They were terrified and asked each other, 'Who is this? Even the wind and the waves obey him!'"*

It's all too easy for us to look calm on the outside while a storm rages on the inside. It's easy to put on a smile – and pretend. But sometimes the greatest fear – the greatest doubt – comes after the storm.

The Gospel writer wants us to know that Jesus cares. He wants us to know Jesus understands what we're feeling.

But Mark also wants us to know the root of fear is a lack of faith. They asked, *"Teacher, don't you care ...?"* and *"Who is this?"* To those disciples, the answer to their question of who Jesus was should have been plain. But it was not. Even the wind and the rain knew who Jesus was, and they obeyed him! *Mark wants us to see who Jesus is.*

TRAINING WHEELS

It seems like just yesterday that we took the training wheels off my youngest daughter's bike. Because Cashmira had been riding on the bike *with* training wheels for almost two years, it was not that difficult for her to make the transition to a bike without them. In just three days she was able to ride the bike without the aid of my wife or my oldest daughter.

Then it happened. She was experimenting with her new found freedom, proud of the fact she was able to be a "big girl." She took a spill and scraped her chin, cheek, and wrist.

It was just after supper when she fell off the bike. She cried herself to sleep after her bath while recalling the incident to my wife. I went to her room and asked her what was wrong. "I want the training wheels back on!" she cried, covering her face with her blanket.

When fear overcomes me, when doubt pervades my circumstances, I find myself telling my Father the same thing: "I want the training wheels back on!"

"No, Lord. You're going too fast for me. Can I take one step backward? Can I rest in what I can see? I'm not sure I want to move ahead. I'm scared! *I want the training wheels back on!*" And I cover my head with my blanket.

How about you? Do you find yourself asking if God cares? Why are you so afraid? Do you still have no faith?

∽✺∼

Do you find yourself asking if God cares? Does God really care?

∽✺∼

Does God really care? It's a question of trust. Just ask Cashmira. Take off the training wheels, and a few scrapes and bruises later she was riding with her friends.

When God our Father sends a storm, it shouldn't matter whether we're awake or sleeping. *Jesus wasn't worried because he knew who sent the storm.*

Does God really care? It's a question of trust. Ask yourself who's sending the storms. **"Why are you so afraid? Do you still have no faith?"**

Prayer

My Father, it's easy to think that you are asleep in my life – that you do not care. Thank you for this reminder from the life of the disciples that you have command not only over the spiritual world, but the physical world as well. Whenever I fool myself into thinking you are not with me, I ask that you gently remind me that you are in control of my life. Amen.

Talking Points

1. During stormy times in our life, it's easy to think that God doesn't care or is not aware of what we are going though. Why do we sometimes feel as if God is asleep during these difficult trials?

2. *God uses the circumstances of life to teach us about who he is, who we are, and to build our faith in him. Although we wish we could avoid these lessons from God, is there any better way to build our relationship in him? Why or why not?*

11

CAN GOD BE TRUSTED?
The Question of Faith

Immediately Jesus made the disciples get into the boat and go on ahead of him to the other side, while he dismissed the crowd. After he had dismissed them, he went up on a mountainside by himself to pray. When evening came, he was there alone, but the boat was already a considerable distance from land, buffeted by the waves because the wind was against it.

During the fourth watch of the night, Jesus went out to them, walking on the lake. When the disciples saw him walking on the lake, they were terrified. "It's a ghost," they said, and cried out in fear.

But Jesus immediately said to them: "Take courage! It is I. Don't be afraid."

"Lord, if it's you," Peter replied, "tell me to come to you on the water."

"Come," he said. Then Peter got down out of the boat, walked on the water and came toward Jesus. But when he saw the wind, he was afraid and, beginning to sink, cried out, "Lord, save me!"

Immediately Jesus reached out his hand and caught him. **"You of little faith,"** *he said,* **"why did you doubt?"**
~Matthew 14:22-31

The events surrounding this question of Jesus have some similarities to the question we examined in the last chapter. Both occur at *night*. And both events place the disciples in the *middle* of the Sea of Galilee *during a storm*.

But in the last chapter, Jesus is *in* the boat. In this chapter, he's *outside*; outside the boat, that is, because he stayed behind to pray. But take note that Matthew doesn't focus on Jesus' prayer. He focuses on the disciples in the boat.

The Romans divided the night (from sunset to sunrise) into four "watches," the fourth watch being the last before sunrise. During these watches, they posted guards in various places to take turns staying awake at night. Matthew tells us that during this fourth watch the boat was *buffeted by the waves*.

The story is simple: during the storm the disciples spot someone coming out to them across the water. Thinking it is a ghost, they cry out. Now before you forget, let me remind you that these disciples are fishermen. I have no problem believing the storm attributed to their fear because at my house when storms come, it doesn't take long before we find an extra body or two in bed with us!

Jesus assures the disciples that it is he who is coming toward them. Peter decides he's going to see if it *really is* Jesus. *"Lord, if it's you, tell me to come to you on the water."* Jesus simply says, "Come." And Peter jumps out of the boat and into history.

A ROOFTOP EXPERIENCE

A few weeks ago, I borrowed our neighbor's extension ladder and cleaned out all the gutters on our century-old Victorian house. Just before I finished, Arriana came out to watch.

"Dad, can I climb up the ladder?" she asked.

"Sure," I said. And with that, she carefully climbed the ladder to the second story of the house.

No sooner had she gotten to the top, however, then she began coming back down. "What's the matter?" I asked.

"I looked down!" she replied.

Perhaps Peter looked down. What happens to him next is as tragic as the walking on the water is miraculous. He takes his eyes off Jesus and puts them on the storm. And then he begins to sink.

Sometime shortly after 'No,' each child learns to effectively use the word "*why.*" In answer to your bidding to pick up the toys, comes the question, "*Why?*" Every parent knows, even the most carefully crafted response will invoke still further the question, "*Why?*" Just when we think we can take no more, we hear again that innocent and innocuous, "*Why?*"

As we grow older, we learn that "*Why?*" in one context may not mean quite the same thing the other "*Why?*" on a different occasion may mean. And so, "*Why did you leave the refrigerator door open?*" differs greatly from "*Why is the checkbook short $500?*"

Our English translation of the original Greek simply says, "***why did you doubt?***" *Why?* Unfortunately it doesn't carry the full import of what Jesus is asking here. There's more than one way to ask "*why?*" in Greek, and Jesus is *not* asking what *purpose* it served for Peter to doubt. Had Jesus wanted to know what caused Peter to doubt, any of the disciples could have answered the question: the storm, the waves, the darkness, the water, all put fear into Peter. And, therefore, he doubted.

Instead, Jesus uses the more uncommon "*why?*" He wanted to know what *purpose* it served for Peter to doubt. Not, "*What caused you to doubt?*" but, "*What did you accomplish by doubting?*" That was a question only Peter could answer.

"*Why did you doubt?*"

Jesus' inquiry concerned not how a nighttime storm could cause a seasoned fisherman to sink in the waves, but rather if Peter accomplished something useful by doubting!

"*What purpose, Peter, did it serve you to doubt? Was there any advantage?*"

IT'S AS EASY AS 1-2-3!

Arriana, our unicycle rider, has taught millions of neighborhood kids to ride their two-wheeled bikes. And I learned something very interesting from *watching* her teach someone else to ride a bike. As long as the person you're teaching *thinks* you're walking right behind them, they do fine. But as soon as they look back and discover you've let go five steps back, they fall down!

In such a case, our doubt only demonstrates to others how little faith we possess. And we're no different than Peter. The moment we take our eyes off Jesus, the storm around us grabs our attention. And we start to doubt.

⊙℘℘⊙

The only thing we accomplish by our doubt is showing others how little faith we have.

⊙℘℘⊙

DON'T LET GO!!!

I'll never forget how my youngest son, Chase, innocently illustrated this in his life a few years ago in the hallway of our apartment in Virginia Beach.

He was pulling me down the hall as only a 20-month-old can do. Now, I want you to picture this clearly: *I'm following him because he's got me by the hand.* Yet, as he's pulling me along he keeps looking back to see if I am there! *He knows I am there because he's got a hold of my hand!* Yet, he still finds he needs reassurance that his daddy hasn't somehow slipped away.

Sometimes I feel that I'm just like Chase: in need of assurance that God hasn't somehow slipped away.

But before we think we need more faith, note that it is not *how much* faith we have – Peter certainly had enough to get out of the boat – but *whom* we have our faith in. *Can he be trusted? Can God be trusted?* We come again to the central question.

Yes! He can be trusted. But it's a question of faith. Of one thing we can be sure, whenever our foothold starts to sink, it's not because

God has taken his eyes off us, but because we've taken our eyes off him. Whenever we take our eyes off the Lord, and put them on the circumstances of life, we begin to doubt our ability to do what he has called us to do.

ⓒⓔⓒⓞ

Whenever our foothold starts to sink, it's not because God has taken his eyes off us, but because we've taken our eyes off him.

ⓒⓔⓒⓞ

"Why did you doubt?" He asks me the same question. "What purpose does it serve to doubt?" None!

And one other thing. Have you thought how Peter got back into the boat? Matthew tells us that the wind didn't die down until they climbed back into the boat. He also tells us that Jesus took Peter by the hand; Jesus did not carry Peter. In other words, Peter had to walk back on his own. Jesus gave him help and security, but the lesson had not concluded for Peter. Peter still needed to face his doubts and fears.

Jesus showed Peter he didn't have to face those fears alone. Jesus could easily have carried Peter back to the boat, or made the boat come to them, or held Peter up while the disciples rowed the boat over to them, or any number of different things.

But the only way for Peter to benefit was for him to walk back to the boat. And on the return trip you can be sure Peter never took his eyes off Jesus!

The writer to the Hebrews says, "Let us fix our eyes on Jesus, the author and perfecter of our faith."[56]

Can God be trusted? It's a question of faith. What purpose will it serve you to doubt?

Prayer

It's all too easy, Father, to take my eyes off you. Deep down inside I know it doesn't serve any purpose. And yet somehow when the circumstances of life seem to suck me in, I, like Peter, sink under the

*pressure. Help me, Lord, to keep my eyes on you. After all, what purpose
is there in doubting you? Help me, Lord. Amen.*

Talking Points

*1. These last two chapters have focused on God's trust and our
faith. Psychologists tell us that "why" questions are the most penetrating
of any question we can be asked or can ask. When Jesus asked Peter
"why?" he cuts to the heart of the problem in Peter's life. In your own
words, in what was Peter's fear rooted?*

*2. We've all doubted God at one time or another. Our tendency is
to blame God or others for our lack of faith. Why?*

12

WILL GOD EVER LEAVE ME?
The Question of Abandonment

At the sixth hour darkness came over the whole land until the ninth hour. And at the ninth hour Jesus cried out in a loud voice, **"Eloi, Eloi, lama sabachthani?"** *– which means,* **"My God, my God, why have you forsaken me?"**
When some of those standing near heard this, they said, "Listen, he's calling Elijah."
One man ran, filled a sponge with wine vinegar, put it on a stick, and offered it to Jesus to drink. "Now leave him alone. Let's see if Elijah comes to take him down," he said.
With a loud cry, Jesus breathed his last.
The curtain of the temple was torn in two from top to bottom. And when the centurion, who stood there in front of Jesus, heard his cry and saw how he died, he said, "Surely this man was the Son of God!"
-Mark 15:33-39

A few years ago Johnna and I were sitting at a red light in the center lane of a five-lane highway waiting to turn into a shopping center. Traffic on both sides of us whizzed past. We watched with astonishment as a woman carrying two bags of groceries attempted to cross all five lanes. One. Two. Three. As she crossed the fourth lane, I saw out of the corner of my eye the red blur of a compact car come from behind us. I watched as the car knocked shopper and groceries through the air across the fifth lane onto the grass beside the road. *While Johnna covered her face, I cried out!*[57]

Have you ever cried out? If you've ever stubbed your toe on something, you've cried out! But have you ever really cried out? I mean, *really cried out?*

"My God, my God, why have you forsaken me?" By far the most emotional question Jesus ever asked. By far the most intriguing. It's one of the seven "last words" or "sayings" of Jesus as he hung on the cross. Of all the sayings, this is the only one recorded in two Gospels. And it's the only *question* which Jesus asks from the cross.

It's a quotation of Psalm 22. The words of the first two verses of the psalm vividly portray the crucifixion of Jesus. *"My God, my God, why have you forsaken me? Why are you so far from saving me, so far from the words of my groaning? O my God, I cry out by day, but you do not answer, by night, and am not silent."*[58]

F-A-T-H-E-R

In this question from the Cross, Jesus refers to the Father as *"God."* Yet just moments earlier, in his first "word" from the cross, Jesus cried out *"Father, forgive them, for they do not know what they are doing."*[59] And moments after, just before he dies, Jesus will cry out with a loud voice, *"Father, into your hands I commit my spirit."*[60]

In the Garden of Gethsemane, Jesus agonized over what was to come. He cried out, *"Abba Father ... take this cup from me ..."*[61] A second time in the Garden he prayed, *"My Father, if it is not possible for this cup to be taken away unless I drink it, may your will be done."*[62]

More than 150 times during his ministry Jesus called God *Father.* The Pharisees never called Yahweh *Father.* The Sadducees never called God *Father.* The scribes never called God *Father.* Forty times Jesus not only called God *Father,* but *my Father.*

But now, in the unnatural black of midday, Jesus doesn't call the Father *"Father."* He doesn't; he can't.

At that moment in time, Jesus was separated from God the Father. And all of God's wrath was poured out on the Son.

Jesus didn't cry out because of the nails. He didn't cry out because of the pain or the insults. He cried out because of the separation.

"My God, my God, why have you forsaken me?" Do you ever wonder – ever fear – God will forsake you? Leave you? Have you ever feared that maybe, just maybe, God will not be there when you need him most?

Do you ever wonder – ever fear – God will forsake you?

DON'T GO AWAY!

My youngest daughter, Cashmira, usually asks either her mom or me to sit with her when she's falling asleep at night. I volunteered one night because Johnna was folding laundry.

As I sat on the corner of her bed, her eyes met mine. "Daddy," she said, "when I close my eyes and fall asleep, don't go away." What she said gripped my heart. "I won't," I answered.

"My God, my God, why have you forsaken me?" *Jesus asked.*

We can take comfort in the knowledge that Jesus did not ask the question for his own benefit but rather for *our* benefit. Jesus did not ask the question for his own benefit but for the benefit of *you and me*. Jesus never asked a question because he needed to know the answer. Jesus hung on the cross for *you*. Jesus asked the question for *your* sake. *"God made him who had no sin to be sin for us, so that in him we might become the righteousness of God."*[63]

The third verse of Psalm 22 contains the answer to Jesus' question: *"Yet you are enthroned as the Holy One; you are the praise of Israel."* God is holy! It is because God is holy that he forsook his only begotten Son. *"... God so loved the world that he gave his one and only Son, that whoever believes in him shall not perish but have eternal life."*[64]

Mark tells us the people had forsaken Jesus.[65] Jesus was forsaken by his disciples when he was arrested in the Garden.[66] He was forsaken by Peter when Peter denied him.[67] He was forsaken by Judas when Judas betrayed him.[68] And now he is forsaken by the Father.

The answer to Jesus' question is simple. Why? *Because while he became sin for us, the Father looked away.* And the temporary sting of a stubbed toe on the foot of a bed pales in comparison to the pain of the *Great Abandonment.*

Although I wanted to sit the entire night at my daughter's side, I'm not God.

Will God ever forsake us? While it is true that God the Father looked away while God the Son took on our *sin,* we don't need to worry that God will look away from us when we sin. Jesus died for our sin. He died so we wouldn't have to. He was forsaken so we would not be. The separation from the Father Jesus endured was not a separation a child of God ever need worry about. Paul, writing in the Letter to the Romans, assured us,

"I am convinced that neither death nor life, neither angels nor demons, neither the present nor the future, nor any powers, neither height nor depth, nor anything else in all creation, will be able to separate us from the love of God that is in Christ Jesus our Lord."[69]

Will God ever leave us?

One of the last things Jesus promised his followers before his ascension into heaven was that he would never leave them. If you know Jesus as your Savior, he promises you, *"I will never leave you; never will I forsake you. I am with you always, to the very end of the age."*[70]

Prayer

Father, what a comfort knowing I can call you "Father." It's a good feeling knowing you will never leave me nor forsake me. No matter what I do, you will never turn your back on me. No matter what goes on in my life, I have confidence in knowing you will always be with me. When life is bleak, you won't leave me to myself. Thanks for being an ever present help in time of need. Thanks for being my Heavenly Father. Amen.

Talking Points

1. When we do something we know displeases God, it's easy to think God may leave us. While he is not pleased with our sins, why can we be assured God will not abandon us?

2. Maybe you don't have a relationship with God such that you feel comfortable calling him "Father." God desires that we see him as our Father. If you have a Bible, turn to Matthew 6:9-13 and pray the prayer you find there. (If you don't have a Bible, turn to the footnote at the end of this sentence.)[71]

13

WHY HAS GOD LET ME DOWN?
The Question of Perspective

Now that same day two of them were going to a village called Emmaus, about seven miles from Jerusalem. They were talking with each other about everything that had happened. As they talked and discussed these things with each other, Jesus himself came up and walked along with them, but they were kept from recognizing him.

*He asked them, "**What are you discussing together as you walk along?**"*

They stood still, their faces downcast. One of them, named Cleopas, asked him, "Are you only a visitor to Jerusalem and do not know the things that have happened there in these days?"

*"**What things?**" he asked.*

"About Jesus of Nazareth," they replied. "He was a prophet, powerful in word and deed before God and all the people. The chief priests and our rulers handed him over to be sentenced to death, and they crucified him; but we had hoped that he was the one who was going to redeem Israel. And what is more, it is the third day since all this took place. In addition, some of our women amazed us. They went to the tomb early this morning but didn't find his body. They came and told us that they had seen a vision of angels, who said he was alive.

Then some of our companions went to the tomb and found it just as the women had said, but him they did not see."

*He said to them, "How foolish you are, and how slow of heart to believe all that the prophets have spoken! **Did not the Christ have to suffer these things and then enter his glory?**" And beginning with Moses and all the Prophets, he explained to them what was said in all the Scriptures concerning himself.*

~Luke 24:13-27

We sometimes get the idea the only people who really cared about Jesus were some of the better known disciples such as Peter and Andrew, James and John, and the women who followed him closely such as Mary and Mary Magdalene, and Mary[72] and Martha, and perhaps some others.

This passage lets us know *there were others who cared about Jesus.* Not everyone wanted him dead – as the Pharisees did. Not everyone was looking forward to meeting him for the sole purpose of seeing him do a miracle – as Pilate did.[73] Not everyone cast lots for his clothes – as the soldiers at the Cross did.[74]

This passage lets us know these two disciples on the road to Emmaus cared. Overwhelmed by the death of Jesus, they felt as if Jesus let them down.

When he first joins them, his first question stops them dead in their tracks. **"What are you discussing together as you walk along?"** They can't believe anyone could be *unaware* of the dramatic events of this weekend.

PITY PARTY

Do you ever feel everyone else is asleep? Have you ever felt as if you were the only one who was *aware*? Have you ever felt as if you were the only one who *cared*? I know you have. I've been there too! It's a dangerous place to be ... because when we begin believing it, we indulge in a pity party. As a result, we begin to look *inward* instead of *outward and upward.*

"What things?" *he asked.*

"About Jesus of Nazareth," they replied. "He was a prophet."

These two disciples have the right facts concerning Jesus. They just don't have *all* the facts about him. Jesus *was a prophet*, but he was more than that. They weren't wrong about who Jesus was; they just didn't have the complete picture of him.

You see, these disciples didn't count on Jesus dying! He was going to set up his Kingdom ... he was going to make Israel the most glorious nation on the face of the earth. He wasn't supposed to die! They didn't count on that!

If Jesus was a prophet, why didn't they believe him when he said he was going to suffer and die?

GREAT EXPECTATIONS

We all have expectations. Some of us have expectations for *ourselves*. For example, we may expect to lose 20 pounds this year before we have to break out our summer swimsuit.

Some of us, on the other hand, have expectations for *other* people. Some of us have expectations for our in-laws, and our friends, and our neighbors, and our pastor. Some of us expect our son or daughter to choose the right person to marry. Some of us are expecting that our spouse will be faithful.

The reality is that many times we don't live up to our own expectations, and neither do other people.

And it stands to reason that not only do we have certain expectations for ourselves and others, but we have certain expectations of God. And sometimes God doesn't live up to our expectations.

FIELD OF DREAMS

"If you build it, he will come." Those words came to Ray Kinsella in the movie *Field of Dreams*. He listened. He built a baseball field in the middle of his cornfield in late summer the same year.

"Plant a church." Those are the words that came to my wife and me – not audibly, but nonetheless we knew it was of God. We

listened. We planted a church. From day one, it experienced phenomenal growth. In less than a year, it grew close to one hundred fifty.

Through a series of unfortunate events we found ourselves standing on the outside a half year later. What was God doing? Hadn't he asked us to start the church? Hadn't we been obedient? Had we misunderstood God? We struggled with disappointment. Why did God let us down? How unfair! *God did not live up to our expectations.* Do you ever find yourself at that place?

LET DOWN BY GOD

Have you counted on God for something only to have you feel as if he let you down? Have you put all your faith in the fact that God was going to come through for you, and he didn't? *What if God doesn't live up to your expectations?*

That's what happened to the two disciples on the road to Emmaus. Jesus didn't live up to their expectation of what the Messiah should be; his actions didn't match their expectations.

Jesus' suffering was not in their plans. *The Messiah had to suffer and die.*

The truth of the matter is that how we look at something defines our expectations. And conversely, our expectations can define our perspective.

If God does not live up to your expectations, it is probably because you don't have his perspective.

JESUS LOVES ME THIS I KNOW

A few years ago while I studied for my doctorate in one room of the house, Christian and Arriana were in the master bedroom jumping around on our bed. And as they jumped, they sang the children's song, "Jesus Loves Me." Except they weren't singing exactly as you may have learned it. The song is written: "Jesus loves me, this I know: *for* the Bible tells me so." But they were singing, "Jesus loves me, this I know, *all* the Bible tells me so."

I went in there and with my B.S. in Bible, my masters in theology, and my *almost doctorate* in ministry, and I began to tell them they had it *all* wrong. But once I got there and listened to them, the longer I thought about it, all I could do was walk back out of the room! They were right: *all* the Bible tells me about Jesus. "... *he explained to them what was said in all the Scriptures concerning himself.*"

Imagine. Saddened over the loss of Jesus, these two disciples leave Jerusalem and walk the whole way to Emmaus with him and never realize it. These disciples can't believe this stranger does not know what has transpired in Jerusalem.

ಞಞಞ

Isn't it ironic that Jesus is the only one who does know what is going on?

ಞಞಞ

But isn't it ironic that Jesus is the only one who does know what is going on? Jesus is the only one who knows more completely the events of the last few days than anyone else, including these two!

How often do we fool ourselves into thinking Jesus doesn't know what we're going through at home? How often do we feel Jesus doesn't know what we're going through at work? How often do we feel Jesus doesn't know what we're going through with our spouse? How often do we feel Jesus doesn't know what we're going through with our kids? How often do we feel Jesus doesn't know what we're struggling with?

It's easy for us to think God doesn't care how we feel, that he's unaware of what we are going through, that he's not *there*. But Jesus knows your situation, Jesus knows your need. Jesus knows you completely.

The question is, *Do you have his perspective?* The best way to get God's perspective on something is to know God. Walk with him. Sit down with him with your open Bible. Listen to him. He'll speak to you. He'll open your eyes, and he'll open your heart, and he'll open your mind.

On the road that day the Prophet of All Prophets, the very Living Word of God, opened the Scriptures to them as it had never been opened before. *"And beginning with Moses and all the Prophets, he explained to them what was said in all the Scriptures concerning himself."*

God hasn't let you down. *It's a question of perspective.*

Prayer

Lord, I confess that I need to take a walk with you to Emmaus. I need to hear things from your perspective. It is easy, Lord, to put my expectations on you — expectations that are selfish and revolve around our agenda. But as the prophet Isaiah reminds me, "my thoughts are not your thoughts, neither are your ways my ways, declares the LORD."[75] *Reveal yourself to me, Lord, every day. Walk with me, Lord, in a way I may never have experienced before. Amen.*

Talking Points

1. We all have expectations of others — including God. Why is our perspective of God defined in part by our expectations of who he is to us and what he can do for us?

2. We can get God's perspective from reading God's Word and from praying. Are there other ways to gain a heavenly perspective?

EPILOGUE

I'll never forget the day my oldest son, Christian, asked me where heaven was. At the time, he was nine years old.

Search the pages of Scripture and you won't find Jesus asking that question. He knew where heaven was. "I go to prepare a place for you," Jesus said, "and if I go and prepare a place for you, I will come back and take you to be with me that you also may be where I am."[76] He knows, but he's not telling.

I told my son I thought it was up. What would you have said?

On later reflection I thought to myself that heaven is anywhere that Jesus is; that's what Jesus said – "that you also may be where I am." Heaven is the comfort we feel when hurt surrounds us. Heaven is the peace we know when anxiousness threatens to overwhelm us. Heaven is the joy we experience when sadness pervades our thoughts.

Where's heaven? That's one question Jesus didn't ask. It's one question we'll have to ask him. Someday. Until then, I'll stick with the answer I gave my son.

Chris Bozung
October 2012

Postscript

There have been more than a few changes since I first began writing this book. Christian is now twenty. Arriana is nineteen. Cashmira is fifteen and Chase is a "big" twelve.

Time has a way of moving us forward and forcing changes upon us that we wouldn't otherwise want or (perhaps, more likely), would not expect. For example, my parents sold both the Pennsylvania homestead of 35 years and their winter home in Florida. They now live in Colorado permanently.

As for Johnna and me – for the first time in twenty-five years, we're not planning to return to our usual fishing ground. Time. It marches on. The questions of Jesus? They're timeless, unchangeable, forever.

About the Author

Christopher Bozung holds a B.S. in Bible from *Philadelphia Biblical University,* a *Th.M. from Dallas Theological Seminary,* a D.Min. from *Regent University,* and studied for a year at *Jerusalem University College* in Jerusalem, Israel. He has been involved in ministry for over 35 years as a pastor, teacher, and church planter. His passion is to know the Savior more deeply and to teach others to know him. He lives with his wife, Johnna, in Marion, Iowa where they home school their four children.

ACKNOWLEDGEMENTS

This book would not have been made possible without the help of countless individuals who read it in various stages:

To those whom I met while at *Regent University*, Virginia Beach, Virginia: Marcus Ryan, Pam Conner, Burt Matteson, Scott DuPont, John Halstead, Kristin Coté, Raquel Werk, Ejukwa Osam, Matt Garnett, Sandra Crabtree, and Joshua Childers. Dr. Russell West and Dr. Wie Liang Tjiong for being a part of my doctoral project. Thanks.

To friends from Pennsylvania to Florida, from Texas to England: Sherri Thomas, Karn Monson, Kimn Gollnick, Celeste Gossman, Ed Dickerson, and Conrad Gempf. I am indebted to all of you.

To the adult Sunday school class at *Trinity Bible Church* in Richardson, Texas: thank you for allowing me to test the concept for this book during our Sunday morning classes.

To Grady Gulliver, Joan Carey, and John O'Brien at *Potter's Hand Community Fellowship*, Catawissa, Pennsylvania: my sincere thanks for your encouragement and support.

To those at *Grace Bible Church*, Virginia Beach, Virginia, and various churches in the greater Cedar Rapids, Iowa area – thanks for listening to this book via my Sunday messages. To Michael Langer and Rita Parks – thanks for reading the manuscript. And thanks Ed Smith for technical help.

To my brother Doug, and sisters Jen and Sharlene.

To my mom and dad, and especially my dad for much of the proofreading on the technical aspects of the book.

A special thanks to Blane and Joan Wollschlager, Ron and Nina Kohler, Jim and Michelle Klinedinst, Dave and Nancy Malone, Ken and Linda Miller, Dr. Cretsinger and Dr. Cuhel, and Dave and Sue Helm. You have helped us live the questions of Jesus.

Thank you, too, to my publishers Henry and Jody Neufeld.

Finally, to my wife Johnna and children Christian, Arriana, Cashmira, and Chase. Without your patience, understanding, and encouragement this book would not have been written. I love you.

NOTES
(ENDNOTES)

1   *Newsweek, March 23, 1992, 21.*

2   Paul F. Boller, Jr., *Presidential Anecdotes (New York: Oxford University Press, 1981), p. 283.*

3   Matthew 1:20-21 and Luke 1:26-38

4   Matthew 2:1-12

5   Luke 1:26-38

6   Colossians 1:16

7   Mark 3:21

8   John 7:5

9   Mark 6:17

10   Mark 12:12

11   Mark 14:1

12   Mark 14:46

13   Acts 26:24

14   Matthew 12:49

15   2 Timothy 3:12

16   Although this question is a statement in the NIV, the Greek sentence construction allows for either a statement or a question.

17   Psalm 15:1-5

18   Genesis 25:27-34; 27:1-45

19   Luke 23:8

20   Luke 23:9

21   Judges 6:34-40

22   Judges 6:36

23   John 20:29

24   Mark 11:24

25   John 2:12

26   Luke 1:26-38

27   Matthew 1:20-24

28   Luke 2:8-14

29   Luke 2:15-18

30   Matthew 2:1-11
31   Luke 2:41-51
32   1 Peter 5:7
33   Psalm 46:10
34   John 14:1
35   Psalm 37:7
36   You may have noticed that your version doesn't contain verse 4, while some of you may be reading a version of the Bible that contains verse 4. Verse 4 reads as follows, "and they waited for the moving of the waters. From time to time and angel of the Lord would come down and stir up the waters. The first one into the pool after each such disturbance would be cured of whatever disease he had."

Our best, earliest, and the most reliable translations of the Bible do not contain verse 4 before the second century A.D. Most Bible scholars agree it is not part of the original version of John's Gospel, and it was most likely added as an explanation of what the invalid says in verse 7 when he says to Jesus, **"I have no one to help me into the pool when the water is stirred. While I am trying to get in, someone else goes down ahead of me."**

Evidently, someone around the 2nd century thought the text needed a little more explanation, and added verse 4 to shed some light on verse 7. But our most reliable copies of the Bible don't contain it, and so I'm content to treat it as an addition to the original text.

Whatever the explanation, whatever the man believes, really doesn't matter. The invalid may have truly believed that an angel came from time to time to stir the waters.

So whether it is part of the original text or not doesn't change or diminish Jesus' words to the invalid.

37   Many of these gate-names can be found in Nehemiah 2-3.
38   Nehemiah 3:1, 32; 12:39
39   Long after the invalid picked up his mat and walked away, the Romans continued using the pool of Bethesda as a health center. If you travel just inside the northeast corner of Jerusalem to a quiet little church by the name of *Saint Anne,* you can see the pool. It's still there. It's not filled with water, though. In fact, most of it is covered over with dirt. A sad memorial to the miraculous gift imparted to a bewildered beneficiary one Sabbath day.

If you travel just outside the northwest corner of Washington, D.C., you can visit another place of healing – the National Naval Medical Center. It's located in another Bethesda – Bethesda, Maryland. A community of some 65,000 people. In fact, the National Institutes of Health and the National Library of Medicine are all located in Bethesda, Maryland. Bethesda was named after a church by the same name built in the 1820s. And you know where they got *that name.*

40   Numbers 20
41   Jonah 3:10-4:1
42   Genesis 4:1-16
43   Genesis 37
44   The woman becomes the man in the parable who had been forgiven a great debt. But be careful, the comparison stops there. Simon is not the man who has been forgiven a small debt, because he has not experienced the forgiveness of God.
45   Luke 5:19
46   Deuteronomy 28:21-22; 27-29; 35; John 9:1-2
47   Psalm 103:3; 147:3; 1 Samuel 19:22
48   Luke 5:17
49   John 13:36-38
50   John 18:15-27
51   Mark 1:17
52   John 11:35
53   Luke 19:41
54   Mark 14:34
55   Hebrews 4:15-16
56   Hebrews 12:2
57   In case you're wondering, she survived the accident.
58   Psalm 22:1-2
59   Luke 23:34
60   Luke 23:46
61   Mark 14:36
62   Matthew 26:42
63   2 Corinthians 5:21
64   John 3:16
65   Mark 14:29
66   Mark 14:50
67   Mark 14:66-72
68   Mark 14:45
69   Romans 8:38-39
70   Hebrews 13:5 and Matthew 28:20
71   'This, then, is how you should pray: "Our Father in heaven, hallowed be your name, your kingdom come, your will be done on earth as it is in heaven. Give us this day our daily bread. Forgive us our debts as we also have forgiven our debtors. And lead us not into temptation, but deliver us from the evil one"' (Matthew 6:9-13).
72   That is, Mary of Bethany and her sister Martha.
73   Luke 23:8
74   John 19:23-24

75   Isaiah 55:8
76   John 14:2-3

ALSO FROM ENERGION PUBLICATIONS

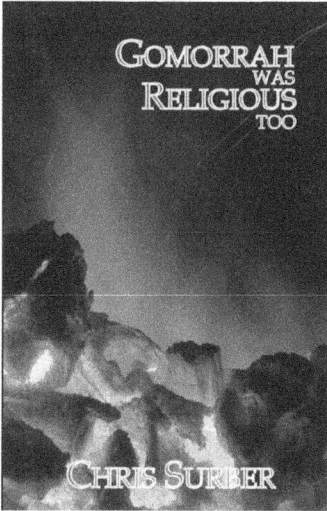

Chris Surber is a prophetic voice issuing an urgent and passionate wake-up call to the Church.

Dr. Harvey R. Brown, Jr.
President
Impact Ministries

Black has done the Church at large and Baptists in particular a great service: if we heed his words we will recover the way of Christ as the only way to live.

Rodney Reeves
Dean, The Courts Redford
College of Theology
and Ministry
Southwest Baptist University

MORE FROM ENERGION PUBLICATIONS

Personal Study

Finding My Way in Christianity	Herold Weiss	$16.99
Holy Smoke! Unholy Fire	Bob McKibben	$14.99
The Jesus Paradigm	David Alan Black	$17.99
When People Speak for God	Henry Neufeld	$17.99
The Sacred Journey	Chris Surber	$11.99

Christian Living

Faith in the Public Square	Robert D. Cornwall	$16.99
Grief: Finding the Candle of Light	Jody Neufeld	$8.99
I Want to Pray	Perry M. Dalton	$7.99
Soup Kitchen for the Soul	Renee Crosby	$12.99
Crossing the Street	Robert LaRochelle	$16.99

Bible Study

Learning and Living Scripture	Lentz/Neufeld	$12.99
From Inspiration to Understanding	Edward W. H. Vick	$24.99
Luke: A Participatory Study Guide	Geoffrey Lentz	$8.99
Philippians: A Participatory Study Guide	Bruce Epperly	$9.99
Ephesians: A Participatory Study Guide	Robert D. Cornwall	$9.99

Theology

Creation in Scripture	Herold Weiss	$12.99
The Politics of Witness	Allan R. Bevere	$9.99
Ultimate Allegiance	Robert D. Cornwall	$9.99
History and Christian Faith	Edward W. H. Vick	$9.99
The Adventists' Dilemma	Edward W. H. Vick	$14.99
The Church Under the Cross	William Powell Tuck	$11.99

Ministry

Clergy Table Talk	Kent Ira Groff	$9.99
Out of This World	Darren McClellan	$24.99

Generous Quantity Discounts Available
Dealer Inquiries Welcome
Energion Publications — P.O. Box 841
Gonzalez, FL 32560
Website: http://energionpubs.com
Phone: (850) 525-3916

www.ingramcontent.com/pod-product-compliance
Lightning Source LLC
Chambersburg PA
CBHW031555040426
42452CB00006B/310